Lecture Notes in Computer Science 8292

Commenced Publication in 1973
Founding and Former Series Editors:
Gerhard Goos, Juris Hartmanis, and Jan van Leeuwen

T0235634

Roderick Bloem   Peter Lipp (Eds.)

Trusted Systems

5th International Conference, INTRUST 2013
Graz, Austria, December 4-5, 2013
Proceedings

 Springer

Volume Editors

Roderick Bloem
Peter Lipp
Graz University of Technology
Institute for Applied Information Processing and Communications
Graz, Austria
E-mail: {rbloem; plipp}@iaik.tugraz.at

ISSN 0302-9743   e-ISSN 1611-3349
ISBN 978-3-319-03490-4   e-ISBN 978-3-319-03491-1
DOI 10.1007/978-3-319-03491-1
Springer Cham Heidelberg New York Dordrecht London

Library of Congress Control Number: 2013951997

CR Subject Classification (1998): D.4.6, E.3, K.6.5, C.2, K.4.4, J.1, H.4

LNCS Sublibrary: SL 4 – Security and Cryptology

Typesetting: Camera-ready by author, data conversion by Scientific Publishing Services, Chennai, India

Printed on acid-free paper

Springer is part of Springer Science+Business Media (www.springer.com)

Preface

This volume contains the papers presented at InTrust13: the 5th International Conference on Trusted Systems held during December 4–5, 2013 in Graz, Austria.

The InTrust conference focuses on the theory, technologies, and applications of trusted systems. It is devoted to all aspects of trusted computing systems, including trusted modules, platforms, networks, services and applications, from their fundamental features and functionalities to design principles, architecture, and implementation technologies. The goal of the conference is to bring academic and industrial researchers, designers, and implementers together with end-users of trusted systems, in order to foster the exchange of ideas in this challenging and fruitful area.

InTrust 2013 built on the four previous successful conferences in the series, held in Beijing in December 2009 (LNCS 6163), December 2010 (LNCS 6802), and November 2011 (LNCS 7222). InTrust 2012 was held at Royal Holloway, London, in December 2012 (LNCS 7711).

This year, InTrust was collocated with ETISS, the 7th European Trusted Infrastructure and Systems School, which had its second visit to Graz. The ETISS topics have a wide overlap with INTRUST covering a variety of fields related to creating a trusted infrastructure to cope with the demands of current and future information processing. Joint ETISS/INTRUST sessions gave ETISS students the chance to listen and talk to top researchers in this field.

We would like to thank the Steering Commitee, in particular Liqun Chen for her help in organizing the conference. We would like to thank Andrei Voronkov for EasyChair and Springer for their help in publishing the proceedings. We are very grateful to the Beijing Institute of Technology for providing the best paper award. The conference would not have taken place but for Martina Piewald, Martin Pirker, and Ronald Toegl.

Finally, we would like to thank the Program Committee members, the sub-reviewers, the authors, and the attendees.

September 2013

Roderick Bloem
Peter Lipp

Organization

Program Committee

Roderick Bloem	Graz University of Technology, Austria
Liqun Chen	HP Laboratories, Bristol, UK
Zhong Chen	Peking University, China
Xuhua Ding	SMU, Singapore
Loic Duflot	ANSSI, France
Dieter Gollmann	Hamburg University of Technology, Germany
Sigrid Gürgens	Fraunhofer Institute for Secure Information Technology, Germany
Stefan Katzenbeisser	TU Darmstadt, Germany
Dirk Kuhlmann	HP Laboratories, Bristol, UK
Xuejia Lai	Shanghai Jiaotong University, China
Mario Lamberger	NXP Semiconductors, Austria
Jiangtao Li	Intel Corporation, USA
Peter Lipp	Graz University of Technology, Austria
Javier Lopez	University of Malaga, Spain
Stefan Mangard	Infineon, Germany
Andrew Martin	University of Oxford, UK
Shin'ichiro Matsuo	NICT, Japan
Chris Mitchell	Royal Holloway, University of London, UK
Yi Mu	University of Wollongong, Australia
Martin Pirker	Graz University of Technology, Austria
Graeme Proudler	HP Laboratories, Bristol, UK
Scott Rotondo	Oracle, USA
Mark Ryan	University of Birmingham, UK
Willy Susilo	University of Wollongong, Australia
Ronald Toegl	Graz University of Technology, Austria
Claire Vishik	Intel Corporation, UK
Jian Weng	Jinan University, China
Marcel Winandy	Ruhr University Bochum, Germany
Xinwen Zhang	Samsung, USA
Yongbin Zhou	Institute of Information Engineering, Chinese Academy of Sciences, China
Liehuang Zhu	Beijing Institute of Technology, China
Yan Zhu	University of Science and Technology Beijing, China

Additional Reviewers

Biedermann, Sebastian
Hiller, Matthias
Jiang, Haiqing

Building Secure Systems with Software-Based Attestation
(Invited Keynote)

Adrian Perrig

Institute of Information Security,
Eidgenössische Technische Hochschule Zürich,
F85.1, CNB F, CH-8092 Zurich, Switzerland
adrian.perrig@inf.ethz.ch

Abstract. Attestation is a promising approach for building secure systems. The recent development of a Trusted Platform Module (TPM) by the Trusted Computing Group (TCG) that is starting to be deployed in common laptop and desktop platforms is fueling research in attestation mechanisms.

In this talk, I will present an alternative approach for attestation that does not rely on trusted hardware called Software-based Attestation. Our approach enables a verifier to obtain the property of untampered code execution on legacy hardware. I will present constructions and applications of Software-based Attestation.

Table of Contents

Session 1: Hardware-Based Security and Applications

Para-Virtualizing the Trusted Platform Module: An Enterprise
Framework Based on Version 2.0 Specification 1
    Jiun Yi Yap and Allan Tomlinson

The PACE|CA Protocol for Machine Readable Travel Documents 17
    Jens Bender, Marc Fischlin, and Dennis Kügler

A Spatial Majority Voting Technique to Reduce Error Rate
of Physically Unclonable Functions 36
    Patrick Koeberl, Jiangtao Li, and Wei Wu

Session 2: Access Control, Integrity and Policy Enforcement

Active File Integrity Monitoring Using Paravirtualized Filesystems 53
    Michael Velten, Sascha Wessel, Frederic Stumpf, and Claudia Eckert

Remote Policy Enforcement for Trusted Application Execution
in Mobile Environments 70
    *Fabio Martinelli, Ilaria Matteucci, Andrea Saracino, and
Daniele Sgandurra*

Towards Policy Engineering for Attribute-Based Access Control 85
    *Leanid Krautsevich, Aliaksandr Lazouski, Fabio Martinelli, and
Artsiom Yautsiukhin*

Author Index 103

Para-Virtualizing the Trusted Platform Module: An Enterprise Framework Based on Version 2.0 Specification

Jiun Yi Yap and Allan Tomlinson

Information Security Group
Royal Holloway, University of London
Egham, Surrey
TW20 0EX, United Kingdom
Jiun.Yap.2012@live.rhul.ac.uk, Allan.Tomlinson@rhul.ac.uk

Abstract. This paper introduces a framework for para-virtualizing the newer Trusted Platform Module (TPM) version 2.0. The framework covers the design of a para-virtualized TPM 2.0 and the considerations when deploying it for use in an Enterprise Information Technology (IT) infrastructure. To develop this framework, a quick study of the TPM 2.0 specification was undertaken and a survey of para-virtualizing TPM techniques was carried out. The study found that TPM 2.0 core functions are suitable for para-virtualization. A set of requirements was then developed to guide the design of this framework. The framework includes components to support the para-virtualized TPM. The framework also covers external components that are essential for the proper functioning of the para-virtualized TPM in an Enterprise IT environment. Research challenges for this framework are then discussed at the end of the paper.

Keywords: Trusted Platform Module 2.0, Para-Virtualization, Framework, Enterprise IT.

1 Introduction

Virtualization is a fundamental technology that is widely used in Enterprise IT infrastructures. Users of virtualization technology need some level of assurance about the expected behavior of a virtual machine (VM) and its ability to protect confidential information from unauthorized disclosure. The TPM specified by the Trusted Computing Group (TCG) offers security properties that can be leveraged by the users of virtualization technology to increase the protection of the system and data from cyber security threats [1].

However, the TPM was originally designed for use with a computing system in a one to one relationship. In a virtualized system, the design will require enhancements to the TPM in order for it to work in an environment where a computer hardware platform hosts several VM. There are generally two types of technique to enable a TPM hardware chip to support multiple VM. The first type is full virtualization of the

R. Bloem and P. Lipp (Eds.): INTRUST 2013, LNCS 8292, pp. 1–16, 2013.

TPM which is exemplified by the work of Vincent Scarlata et al. [4]. In that paper, the authors described the creation of software virtual TPM instances contained in a privileged VM. Each virtual TPM will support a unique VM. This design is aligned to the virtual TPM framework proposed in TCG's Virtualized Trusted Platform Architecture Specification [5] and Open Trusted Computing's VTPM Architecture [6]. Although the designs often extend the root of trust from the TPM hardware chip to the virtual TPM, the security protection for confidential data provided by the TPM's hardware based protected storage location is not offered. A probable reason could be that these designs are based on the older TPM 1.2 specification and the limited amount of TPM memory is unable to support the requirements of the virtualized environment. In addition, the long chain of trust from the TPM hardware chip to the virtual TPM can be fragile as the attack surface is now wider compared to a non-virtualized implementation.

This paper will analyze the other type of technique which is para-virtualizing TPM. Paul England et al. wrote that TPM para-virtualization refers to the method of mediating guest VM access to hardware TPM using a software component [7]. The design will require no change to most of TPM functionality but some aspects of the device interface may change. A major advantage offered by this technique is the availability of TPM hardware based protected storage location and this feature is desired by organizations that requires hardware based security; for example, government Enterprise IT. Moreover, the chain of trust is now shorter as the VM can access the TPM hardware chip in a more direct manner. However, in a para-virtualization design, the use of the resources belonging to a single TPM by multiple VM has to be managed to ensure fair sharing and prevent cross-interference. On the other hand, the TPM has to provide sufficient resource to support the operation of several VM. With the advent of the newer TPM 2.0 specification, it is timely to examine if the newer specification can better support para-virtualization requirement. This para-virtualization framework will introduce components that leverage on new capabilities offered by TPM 2.0. The framework will also address the challenges for achieving TPM para-virtualization in Enterprise IT, for example, backup and migration.

This is a research paper rather than a presentation of an actual implementation. It contains a quick study of the new TPM 2.0 specification from the TCG and analyzes the state of the art regarding para-virtualizing the TPM. With this background knowledge, the paper will then examine the extent to which TPM 2.0 core functions are suitable for para-virtualizing. This is followed by a proposed framework for para-virtualizing TPM 2.0 in the context of an Enterprise IT infrastructure. The paper will end with a discussion on research challenges for the proposed framework.

2   Introducing TPM 2.0

The Trusted Computing Group (TCG) wrote in the Trusted Platform Module (TPM) version 2.0 specification [2] that trust conveys an expectation of behaviour from the computer system. In other words, a user can trust a computer if it always behaves as it is intended to. The assessment of trust always begins from some baseline, or "root of trust". In a computing platform, the three roots of trust for measurement, storage and reporting provide the minimum functionality required to describe the attributes that contribute towards its trustworthiness. The TPM and supporting components aim to provide these 3 roots of trust.

TPM 2.0 is the latest specification from the TCG and it replaces the previous TPM 1.2 specification. The changes and enhancements to TPM 2.0 compared to the previous TPM version include: support for additional cryptographic algorithms, enhancements to the availability of the TPM to applications, enhanced authorization mechanisms, simplified TPM management and additional capabilities to enhance the security of platform services.

2.1   Architecture

TPM 2.0 is designed to be a self-contained computing device. This allows the TPM device to be trusted to carry out computations without relying on external computing resources. The following are short descriptions of the subsystems in a TPM 2.0 device while detailed explanation can be obtained from TPM 2.0 specification [2].

I/O Buffer – This component enables the host computing system to communicate with the TPM. It can be a shared memory. Data to be processed by the TPM will be validated at this point.

Cryptography Subsystem – The cryptographic engine supports commonly used cryptographic functions like hashing, asymmetric operations such as digital signature and key exchange, symmetric encryption, random number generator and key derivation function. These cryptographic functions can be used by the other TPM components or the host computer.

Authorization Subsystem – Before a TPM command is executed, this subsystem checks that proper authorization data has been given by the calling application.

Volatile Memory – This memory holds transient TPM data, including Platform Configuration Registers (PCR), data objects and session data. PCR contains the integrity measurements of critical components in the host computer. A data object can either be a cryptographic key or other data. The TPM uses sessions to manage the execution of a series of commands.

Non-Volatile (NV) Memory – This memory is used to store persistent TPM data that includes the platform seed, endorsement seed, storage seed and monotonic counter. Additional PCR banks can be created in this memory.

Management Subsystem – This subsystem oversees the operation of the various TPM states. Basic TPM states include power-off, initialization, start up, shut down, self-test, failure and field upgrade.

Execution Engine – This firmware contains the program instructions and data structures that are required to run a TPM command. These program instructions and data structures cannot be altered by the host computing platform. In the event of a firmware upgrade, there are security mechanisms to ensure that the update is authorized and the new firmware is checked for authenticity and integrity.

2.2   Core Functions

A Trusted Computing Base (TCB) can be a BIOS, Virtual Machine Monitor (VMM) or operating system that has proved to be highly secure and hence trustworthy. When a TCB is made to work together with a TPM, they can offer the capabilities of integrity measurement and reporting, protected data storage, certification and attestation and authentication. In integrity measurement, a hash function is performed by the BIOS on the first software component that is started when the computer powers up. The hash function will produce a digest of that software component. If that software component is altered, the digest will be different from the one obtained when the software component was first measured. This digest can be stored in the PCR located in either the volatile or non-volatile memory of the TPM. TrustedGRUB [3] is an application that implements this integrity measurement at system start. A TPM can have an authenticity certificate from the manufacturer and this feature is used in conjunction with the integrity measurement to report the "trustworthiness state" of a computing platform.

A unique feature of the TPM is the use of primary seeds to generate hierarchies of keys for use in cryptographic functions. The intention of this feature is to provide the flexibility to support different types of cryptographic functions without increasing the storage memory requirement. To establish trust in a key derived from a TPM primary seed, the TPM can produce with a certificate indicating that the processes used for creating and protecting the key meet the necessary security requirements. During attestation, a TPM can vouch for the authenticity and properties of either the host computing platform, a piece of software or a cryptographic key.

TPM non-volatile memory is typically used to store cryptographic keys that protect sensitive data. In this method, the sensitive data is encrypted with a cryptographic key derived from a root key inside the TPM chip. This cryptographic key is usually stored into the non-volatile memory of the TPM chip. To read the sensitive data, the user has to provide authorization data to the TPM chip and only upon successful authorization will the cryptographic key be released from the TPM chip. This is known as protected storage.

3   State of the Art for Para-Virtualizing the TPM

The following sub-sections will give brief descriptions of two projects on para-virtualizing TPM. It is important to note that these two projects are based on the older TPM 1.2 specification.

3.1   Para-Virtualized TPM Sharing

In this paper [7], the authors describe a para-virtualization design that allows a VMM to time share a TPM among its VM. The concept of associating a TPM context to a particular VM is proposed. A TPM context will contain the important data that defines a TPM state, for example, keys and sessions. When a particular VM wishes to use the physical TPM, the associated TPM context is loaded into that physical TPM.

The loaded TPM context can be saved and cleared from the physical TPM to allow other TPM context to be loaded when required. TPM contexts are saved in the hypervisor. As a result, the design is able to support most TPM applications.

To implement this design, the authors located the TPM para-virtualization management software in the hypervisor. Figure 1 gives a high level view of this design.

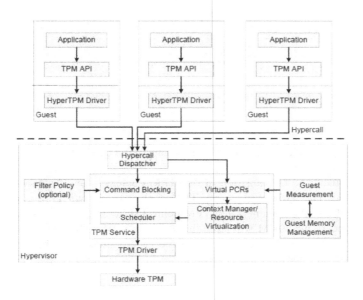

Fig. 1. Architecture for para-virtualizing TPM sharing from [7]

The TPM para-virtualization management software contains the following components:

Scheduler – Rosters shared access to the physical TPM.

Command Blocking – Filters TPM commands based on a pre-determined list of allowed commands. This is to ensure the safe operation of the TPM by disallowing applications in VM from executing certain TPM commands.

Virtual PCR – Each VM is assigned a set of virtual PCR and they are managed by the hypervisor.

Context Manager - This component inspects every TPM command and load the associated context into the physical TPM so that the VM can only access its own TPM resources.

Resource Virtualization – Certain limited TPM resources are virtualized, for example, key slots, authorization session and transport sessions. These virtualized TPM resources are tied to a context that is provided by the context manager.

The use of virtual PCR to store integrity measurements of the VM is not desired by organizations that require hardware based protected storage location. Furthermore, the authors do not elaborate on TPM migration and management of TPM endorsement credentials in this paper.

3.2   Enhancing TPM with Hardware-Based Virtualization Techniques

This paper [8] presented the design of a TPM that supports hardware-based virtualization. In this design, the VMM time multiplexes the hardware TPM in a manner similar to [7]. However, a difference is that the hardware TPM has to be modified to include additional non-volatile memory to store the various TPM contexts. The layout of this multi-context TPM is shown in figure 2.

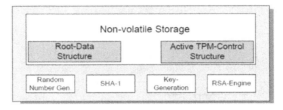

Fig. 2. Layout of the multi-context TPM from [8]

The VMM manages the transition of one TPM context to another using the TPM control structure. The VMM links every TPM context to its own TPM control structure. Figure 3 shows the content of the TPM control structure. When a new TPM context is to be loaded, the VMM will store the previous TPM control structure and load the new TPM control structure. To protect the confidentiality of the TPM control structure, it is encrypted and the cryptographic key is stored in the TPM root data structure.

Fields of the TPM Control Structure
Storage Root Key (SRK)
PCRs [16..23]
Attestation Identity Keys (AIK)
Endorsement Key (EK)
Endorsement Credential
Monotonic Counter Values
Values of the non-volatile storage
Delegation Tables
TPM context data
DAA TPM specific secret (f)
TPM_PERMANENT_FLAGS/DATA
TPM_STCLEAR_FLAGS/DATA
Authorization data

Fig. 3. TPM control structure from [8]

Another difference is the introduction of the concept of protection rings into the TPM. This TPM protection ring has a two level hierarchy that differentiate a privileged TPM mode from a non-privileged TPM mode. The TPM protection ring leverages the Intel VT architecture and hence can be considered as a form of hardware-based protection. There are two forms of CPU operation in the Intel VT architecture. The VMX root operation in which the VMM runs and the VMX non-root operation in which the VM runs. Only VMX root can run the privileged TPM mode while the VMX non-root can only run in the non-privileged TPM mode. In addition, the authors extended the TCG specification for TPM to include extra commands to manage the transition between TPM modes and to control the different TPM contexts. These extra TPM commands can only be executed by VMX root.

For VM migration, the authors described that their TPM context migration protocol is similar to the concept TCG introduced for migratable keys. On TPM credentials, the authors proposed to establish a certificate chain with the root Endorsement Key (EK). For every TPM context, the TPM generates a new EK which is then certified by the root EK. When the TPM context is migrated, the EK will then be re-certified with the root EK of the destination platform.

This design covers many technical aspects of para-virtualizing TPM. However, there are still gaps to cover before this design can be implemented in an Enterprise IT virtualization environment. For example, the support for business continuity plan has to be developed.

4   Examining TPM 2.0 Suitability for Para-Virtualizing

TPM 2.0 core functions are found to be generally suitable for use in a para-virtualized design and only some typical virtualization functions are required at the VMM level to allow a single TPM 2.0 device to support multiple VM. Based on a quick study of TPM 2.0 specification, the extent to which the core functions can be para-virtualized are described in the following paragraphs.

4.1   Endorsement and Storage Keys

Figure 4 shows how the TPM keys can be distributed to multiple VM. An endorsement key is derived from the endorsement primary seed located inside the TPM and it is the basis for the root of trust of reporting. Several endorsement keys can be generated and assigned to the various VM hosted on the computing platform. However, an endorsement key be migrated together with the associated VM. Although this may seem to be unfavorable, attestation, for example, will have to be done again, it is actually better to obtain a new endorsement key after VM migration from the destination TPM since the host computing platform has changed. Meanwhile, a new certificate will have to be obtained for the new endorsement key after VM migration.

For keys derived from the storage root key, they can be created to be migratable by setting the duplication flag. These keys are assigned to the VMs and kept outside the TPM. As an example, when a VM wishes to use the TPM for certification, the certifying key is loaded into the TPM using the command TPM2_Load. At the end of the session, the certifying key is unloaded from the TPM. The TPM can then start a new session with another VM. During VM migration, a certifying key can be packaged as a duplicable data object using TPM2_Duplicate and then migrated over to the designated TPM. TPM2_Import will load the migrated data object into the destination TPM. Meanwhile, the use of a TPM authorization session will ensure that only the

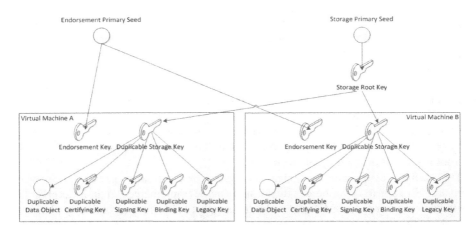

Fig. 4. TPM 2.0 keys distribution for multiple VM

right VM can access its certifying keys. The resulting effect is comparable to the notion of process and resource isolation between VM. Nevertheless, the credential for a
certifying key may have to be re-issued after a migration as the host computer has
changed.

4.2   Protected Storage

There are various TPM 2.0 commands that can move data in and out of either the
volatile or non-volatile memory: for example, TPM2_Load, TPM2_LoadExternal,
TPM2_Unseal, TPM2_NV_Write and TPM2_NV_Read. The use of a TPM authorization data will ensure that only the right VM can access its data in the protected storage location. The mechanism for the migration of these data in protected storage
location is the same as those for certifying keys. For data that are encrypted and the
access control depends on the host computing platform integrity measurements, this
can cause a problem during VM migration when the host computer platform is different. The use of TPM 2.0 Enhanced Authorization will allow a more flexible access
control policy for this type of protected data. For example, the authorization policy
can either check the host platform integrity measurements or other security properties.
In the meantime, the amount of volatile and non-volatile memory has to be managed
to avoid a situation whereby there is insufficient memory for use by all the VM on
that host computer.

4.3   Integrity Measurement and Reporting

TPM2_NV_DefineSpace can be used to create PCR banks in the NV memory.
TPM2_PCR_Extend will then be used to record the integrity measurements
of the VM into the PCR located in the NV memory. For the host machine,
TPM2_PCR_Extend will be used to record the integrity measurements into the PCR

located in the volatile memory. This arrangement will allow the integrity measurement of both the virtual and host machine be stored inside the TPM at the same time. As above, the amount of NV memory has to be managed to avoid the situation whereby there are more VM than the TPM can support. TPM2_Quote is used to report the integrity measurement stored in a particular PCR. When reporting the integrity measurements to a requestor, TPM2_Load is used to insert the relevant attestation key into the TPM. This key is then used to sign the integrity measurement. The mechanisms for the migration and access control of PCR are the same for those for certifying keys.

In addition to the points above, TPM 2.0 is designed with a context management feature that is intended to be used to manage TPM resources among various applications. In a virtualized environment, this feature can instead be used to manage TPM resources among various VM. TPM 2.0 specification states that the structure of the context is decided by the vendor. In other words, there can be a customized context structure to support TPM 2.0 para-virtualization requirements.

As with most hardware virtualization, TPM 2.0 will require some software components at the VMM level to allow it to support multiple VM. For example, a software component is required to provide some form of usage management to ensure that every VM has fair use of the TPM. Another software component is required to block state altering TPM commands issued by non-management VM. The architectures described in TCG's virtualized trusted platform specification [5] are more suited to the full virtualization technique although certain aspects such as TPM migration are applicable to this para-virtualized TPM framework.

5   Requirements for Para-Virtualizing TPM 2.0

As discussed in section 4, TPM 2.0 core functions are generally able to support para-virtualization. However, we noted that there has to be mechanisms to assign and ensure the fair use of TPM resources to multiple VM. In addition, issues pertaining to an Enterprise IT environment, such as migration, certification and logging have to be addressed as well. To this end, the design requirements presented in [1], [4], [7] and [8] were considered and we will like to suggest the following:

1. The way that an application uses the para-virtualized TPM should be the same as for a hardware TPM.
2. The para-virtualized TPM should be always available for use by the VM.
3. Strong association between the VM and its TPM resources. This association should be maintained after the migration of the VM.
4. TPM resources belonging to a VM should not be accessible by another VM.
5. The size of both volatile and non-volatile memory in the TPM should support the additional memory required to host multiple VM on a single physical computer.
6. Data stored in protected storage locations should be preserved unless instructed by their owners. These data should be moved together with the VM during migration and then stored into the protected storage location of the destination TPM.

7. The security strength of protected storage location in a para-virtualized TPM should be the same as for hardware TPM.
8. The activity of the para-virtualized TPM should be logged. The log file associated with a particular VM should be moved to the destination host computing platform during VM migration.
9. Non-privileged VM cannot execute commands that can alter the state of the TPM.
10. The para-virtualized TPM should have verifiable credentials at all times.
11. Individual VM interaction with para-virtualized TPM should be isolated from each other to avoid interference.
12. The para-virtualized TPM should be able to support business continuity plans.

6   An Enterprise Framework for Para-Virtualizing TPM 2.0

The framework shown in figure 5 contains components at the VMM and hardware level to support the para-virtualization of TPM 2.0. This framework allows the multiplexing of TPM 2.0 functions and resources for use by VM and their applications at

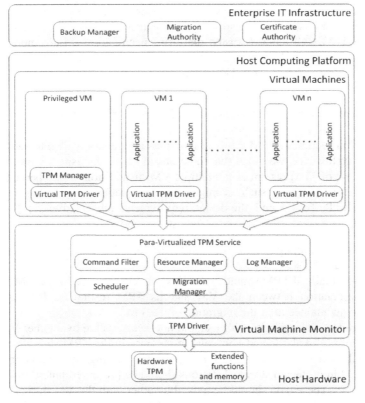

Fig. 5. Enterprise framework for para-virtualizing TPM 2.0

the same time while preserving the hardware based protected storage location. The development of this framework is based on the survey of TPM para-virtualizing works in section 3, the analysis of para-virtualizing TPM 2.0 core functions in section 4 and the design requirements from section 5 of this paper.

As shown in section 4, TPM 2.0 core functions are generally suitable for use in a para-virtualized design. Hence, the software components at the VMM level do not emulate TPM functions but instead focus on ensuring fair usage of TPM and to address requirement such as migration and logging.

A major difference from existing concepts is the removal of virtual PCR as the store for integrity measurements of VM because they will be stored in TPM NV memory. As a result, VM integrity measurements enjoy the security of hardware based protected storage location. In addition, a privileged VM is used to manage the hardware TPM and para-virtualized TPM service. This gives the system administrator a separate conduit to control the hardware TPM and para-virtualized TPM service. There are also provision for TPM hardware enhancements and a log manager. These are security features desired by a high security Enterprise IT infrastructure. Moreover, this framework covers external components that are essential for the proper functioning of the para-virtualized TPM in an Enterprise IT environment. The following paragraphs describe the components in this framework.

6.1   Extended Functions and Additional Memory

The framework allows modifications to be carried out on the TPM hardware to support the requirements of the virtualized environment. For example, the amount of memory can be increased to include more PCR banks to store the integrity measurements of multiple VM. Although hardware modifications can be costly, certain high security requirement, for example, government Enterprise IT, may demand and pay for this enhancement. In addition, the modified hardware can contain extended functions to support new virtualization technique such as the single root I/O virtualization standard specified by the PCI-SIG [12]. Hardware technique such as the use of field-programmable gate array described in [9] can be used to implement the modifications. Depending on security requirements and the amount of modification, a new platform certificate may have to be issued for the modified TPM to vouch that the platform contains a genuine TPM and that the communication path between the TPM and the host computer is trusted.

6.2   Command Filter

As there are commands that can alter the TPM state, for example TPM2_Shutdown, it is necessary that only the TPM manager in the privileged VM can execute such commands. All commands from the VM to the hardware TPM will be inspected and any state altering command from non-privileged VM will be blocked from execution. The command filter can make use of the hardware based virtualization technique described in [8] to enforce the restriction on using selected TPM commands.

6.3   Scheduler

This component sequences VM access to the hardware TPM in a time division multiplexing manner. This will ensure that every VM has an opportunity to use the TPM. The algorithm for sequencing can be either round robin or demand based. In round robin, the scheduler can poll every VM and ask if it likes to use the TPM. Alternatively, the scheduler can arrange access to the TPM whenever the VM makes a request. The time that a VM can use the TPM will be limited. If the TPM is currently servicing a request, any new request will be queued in a first-in-first-out memory cache.

6.4   Resource Manager

To achieve strong association between VM and their TPM resources, the resource manager will administer the assignment of TPM resources such as keys. It is envisioned that the VM will use keys derived from the primary seed in the hardware TPM. In turn, each VM will build their key hierarchy based on their assigned key. Meanwhile, the resource manager will create PCR banks in the TPM NV memory and assign them to the VM. PCR in the TPM volatile memory will be reserved for use by the host computer and VMM. For the purpose of attestation, the resource manager can provide the PCR contents in the TPM volatile memory to the VM. The other task carried out by the resource manager is to work together with the scheduler to isolate the TPM processes and resources of the VM. The mechanisms used to achieve this effect can include the use of TPM context management feature and authorization session. TPM commands such as TPM2_ContextSave, TPM2_ContextLoad, TPM2_FlushContext and TPM2_StartAuthSession will be used. This will prevent one VM from accessing the TPM resources of another VM. TPM contexts are saved in the VMM.

6.5   Migration Manager

During VM migration, this component will work together with the resource manager to oversee the packing of the associated TPM resources into duplicable data objects. The command TPM2_duplicate will be used to prepare the data object for migration. This component will also work with the migration authority to operate a migration protocol that securely moves the duplicated data object to the designated TPM. On the other hand, if the host computer is to receive a migrated VM, the migration manager can carry out the task of authenticating and verifying the trustworthiness of the migrating VM.

6.6   Log Manager

The availability of a log is crucial to forensic investigation in the event of a security incident. The log manager will log down all the operations performed by the VM on the hardware TPM. The log manager can make frequent integrity measurements of the log file and store the measurements in the hardware TPM. This will allow the detection of unauthorized changes to the log file. Meanwhile, the log manager with work together with the migration manager and migration authority to move the log file associated with a particular VM to the destination host computing platform during VM migration.

6.7   TPM Manager

This resides in a privileged VM and is primarily used to manage the hardware TPM and configure the para-virtualized TPM service. The privilege status of this VM can either be enforced from the VMM or controlled by hardware based virtualization technique described in [8]. The TPM manager can check the integrity of the VMM components by querying the hardware TPM.

6.8   TPM and Virtual TPM Driver

The TPM driver contains the software stack that enables the VMM to communicate with the hardware TPM while the Virtual TPM driver contains the software stack that enables the VM to communicate with para-virtualized TPM service in the VMM. To detect unauthorized changes to these two components, integrity measurements are carried out when they are started. The integrity measurements are then stored in the TPM.

6.9   Backup Manager

This and the next two components are external to the computer platform but part of the Enterprise IT infrastructure. To support business continuity planning, the TPM keys for the VM should be archived and stored securely in a physically separate location. In the event of an incident that cause the TPM keys to be lost, the backup TPM keys can be retrieved to support the continuation of business operation.

6.10   Migration Authority

Besides administrating the migration of VM, the migration authority can work with the TPM migration manager to ensure that the accompanying TPM resources are moved to the correct destination TPM.

6.11   Certificate Authority

This component will verify the credentials of TPM keys provided by the VM and issue the appropriate certificates when it is satisfied with the credentials. After a VM has been migrated, it can work with the migration authority to recheck the credentials of the TPM keys and issue new certificates. More importantly, the certificate authority can revoke a particular certificate when required.

7   Requirements Revisited

To assess the thoroughness of the design of this framework, it is compared to the requirements listed in section 5. Firstly, there are no changes to the TPM commands and most TPM commands are available to the VM except for those that can alter TPM state. This meets the requirement of retaining the same TPM usage model. Secondly, the scheduler will sequence the TPM commands issued by the virtual commands. Besides ensuring that every VM can interact with the TPM, it works in conjunction with the resource manager to switch from one VM's TPM session to another session. The resource manager will link the TPM resource to the VM and access control is achieved by using authorization session. The resulting effect is equivalent to isolating each VM's interaction with TPM.

Meanwhile, the migration manager works with the resource manager to maintain the association between a TPM resource and its VM during migration. In addition, this framework allows for modifying the TPM hardware and this provision gives the flexibility to complement TPM hardware with additional memory to meet the TPM memory requirement of multiple VM. TPM 2.0 NV memory is a protected data storage location of this framework. The resource manager can store a certain amount of integrity measurements from numerous VM into this hardware memory. Hence, the security protection of integrity measurement in this para-virtualized TPM is the same as for a plain hardware TPM. The other requirement relating to logging is fulfilled by the log manager while the backup manager is used as part of the business continuity plan. As for certification, this framework uses an external certificate authority to check on the credentials of TPM keys. When it is satisfied with the credentials, it will issue a certificate to vouch for the TPM keys. Last of all, the command filter makes sure that non-privileged VM cannot execute commands that can alter the TPM state. To conclude, this framework meets the requirements set forth in the section 5.

8   Research Challenges

This framework is based on a paper study of TPM 2.0 specification. From the view point of a high level design, this framework can be considered to be reasonable. To validate this framework, the components in the VM monitor have to be implemented and tested. An ideal candidate for the VM monitor is the open source Xen hypervisor [10]. The Xen hypervisor can support para-virtualization and hardware based virtualization technology such as Intel VT and AMD V CPU architecture extension. The hypervisor has a driver for the TPM although it is for TPM 1.2 specification.

The techniques described in [7] and [8] can be redeployed and used to implement this framework but significant challenges still exist. The performance of this para-virtualized TPM design is one area to be investigated further. Research can be carried to develop better algorithms in the scheduler to sequence VM requests for TPM resources. The strength of the isolation between each VM interaction with the para-virtualized TPM is another research area to be studied. The commonly used integrity measurement method of obtaining a digest from hashing a software component can be difficult to implement in a virtualized environment. This is because VM migration can take place and the configuration of host computing platforms can differ. Attestation in such an environment will be tedious as there will be a variety of measurements to contend with. Hence, further research can be under taken to look at other approaches, for example property-based attestation in [11], to obtain a measure of the state of trustworthiness.

The development of use case for this framework is a task not to be neglected. It will be difficult to persuade organizations to take up this framework if there are no functional use scenarios. Meanwhile, threat modeling can be conducted on these scenarios. The results can be used by researchers to harden the design and organizations who wish to adopt the framework can put in mitigation measures recommended from the threat model to avoid the pitfalls. Lastly, the use of TPM monotonic counter by VM is not addressed in the proposed framework and further work can be done to study this matter.

9   Conclusion

The availability of hardware based protected storage location is an advantage that is desired by organizations that require high security for their Enterprise IT infrastructure. This paper found that TPM 2.0 core functions are generally suitable for para-virtualization. This indicates that the technical barrier to using TPM 2.0 in a virtualization environment can be potentially lowered. The proposed framework is holistic as it covers important considerations at different level of the virtualization environment. Differences from existing concepts include storing integrity measurements of VM in TPM NV memory and using a privileged VM to manage the hardware TPM and para-virtualized TPM service. There are also provision for TPM hardware enhancements and a log manager. Moreover, this framework covers external components that are essential for the proper functioning of the para-virtualized TPM in an Enterprise IT environment. To conclude, the studies and framework expressed in this paper provide a comprehensive basis for future work in para-virtualizing TPM 2.0 and integrating the design to an Enterprise IT virtualization environment.

References

1. Scarlata, V., Rozas, C., Wiseman, M., Grawrock, D., Vishik, C.: TPM Virtualization: Building a General Framework. In: Norbert, P., Helmut, R. (eds.) Trusted Computing, pp. 43–56. Vieweg (2007)
2. Trusted Computing Group: Trusted Platform Module Library Family "2.0" Level 00 Revision 00.96, March 15 (2013)
3. TrustedGRUB, http://www.trust.rub.de/projects/trustedgrub/
4. Berger, S., Caceres, R., Goldman, K.A., Perez, R., Sailer, R., van Doorn, L.: vTPM: Virtualizing the Trusted Platform Module. In: Proceedings of the 15th Conference on USENIX Security Symposium, vol. 15, pp. 305–320. USENIX (2006)

5. Trusted Computing Group: Virtualized Trusted Platform Architecture Specification "1.0" Revision 0.26, September 27 (2011)
6. Open Trusted Computing: VTPM Architecture Revision Final 1.0 Update, May 29 (2009)
7. England, P., Loeser, J.: Para-Virtualized TPM Sharing. In: Lipp, P., Sadeghi, A.-R., Koch, K.-M. (eds.) TRUST 2008. LNCS, vol. 4968, pp. 119–132. Springer, Heidelberg (2008)
8. Stumpf, F., Eckert, C.: Enhancing Trusted Platform Modules with Hardware-Based Virtualization Techniques. In: Cotton, A., Dini, O., Skarmeta, A.F.G., Ion, M., Popescu, M., Takesue, M. (eds.) Proceedings of the Second International Conference on Emerging Security Information, Systems and Technologies, SECURWARE 2008, pp. 1–9. IEEE Computer Society (2008)
9. Pirker, M., Winter, J.: Semi-Automated Prototyping of a TPM v2 Software and Hardware Simulation Platform. In: Huth, M., Asokan, N., Čapkun, S., Flechais, I., Coles-Kemp, L. (eds.) TRUST 2013. LNCS, vol. 7904, pp. 106–114. Springer, Heidelberg (2013)
10. Xen Hypervisor, http://www.xenproject.org/
11. Sadeghi, A.-R., Stüble, C., Winandy, M.: Property-Based TPM Virtualization. In: Wu, T.-C., Lei, C.-L., Rijmen, V., Lee, D.-T. (eds.) ISC 2008. LNCS, vol. 5222, pp. 1–16. Springer, Heidelberg (2008)
12. PCI-SIG: Single Root I/O Virtualization and Sharing Specification Revision 1.1, January 20 (2010)

The PACE|CA Protocol for Machine Readable Travel Documents

Jens Bender[1], Marc Fischlin[2], and Dennis Kügler[1]

[1] Bundesamt für Sicherheit in der Informationstechnik (BSI), Germany
[2] Darmstadt University of Technology, Germany

Abstract. The International Civil Aviation Organization (ICAO) has adopted the password-based connection establishment protocol (PACE) for securing the contactless communication between the machine-readable travel documents and the readers at border controls. This Diffie-Hellman based protocol achieves impersonation resistance at password strength. To reinforce authentication of the travel documents beyond this low-entropy security, the challenge-response based active authentication protocol could be executed afterwards. However, this optional protocol is often omitted for efficiency reasons. In order to salvage strong security we investigate the possibility to provide active authentication almost "for free" with the PACE|CA protocol, by re-using some of the randomness from the PACE protocol for authentication.

1 Introduction

The password-based connection establishment protocol (PACE), introduced by the German Federal Office for Information Security in [8], is supposed to protect the contactless communication between identity cards and readers. It is effectively used on the new German identity cards since November 2010. The PACE protocol has also been standardized by the International Civil Aviation Organization (ICAO) through ISO/IEC JTC1 SC17 WG3/TF5 for machine-readable travel documents (MRTDs) when used at border controls.

PACE implements a secure Diffie-Hellman key exchange protocol, allowing the MRTD and the reader to establish a secure channel based on a password provided by the card holder (or deduced from the machine readable zone on the MRTD). As such, PACE helps to secure the subsequent communication, but nonetheless provides "only" a password-based form of authentication and does not, for example, prevent attacks in which the adversary clones cards and guesses the low-entropy password. To ensure stronger forms of authentication and increase the trustworthiness, the ICAO suggests to run the Active Authentication (AA) protocol afterwards in which the card signs a challenge sent by the terminal under a certified key (see Figure 1). This step is, however, costly for the card and only *optional* according to the ICAO 9303 standard [12] for the border control scenario.

R. Bloem and P. Lipp (Eds.): INTRUST 2013, LNCS 8292, pp. 17–35, 2013.

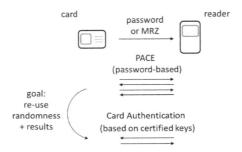

Fig. 1. PACE Protocol for Machine Readable Travel Documents, with additional card authentication. The goal of the proposals PACE|AA, SPACE|AA, and PACE|CA here is to securely re-use randomness and intermediate results from the PACE protocol to speed-up the authentication process.

1.1 Augmenting PACE by Cost-Effective Authentication

To bridge the problem of having to perform the additional authentication step, Bender et al. [5] recently suggested the PACE|AA protocol which combines the PACE and AA protocol steps, saving the card from some of the signature generation steps in AA by re-using the randomness from the PACE part. Roughly, since PACE is a Diffie-Hellman based key exchange protocol their combined protocol works with both Schnorr signatures as well as DSA for the authentications step. Rather than performing a modular exponentiation, a hash computation, and a modular multiplication and addition as for Schnorr signatures computed from scratch, it spares the card the exponentiation by using its contribution to the Diffie-Hellman key from PACE instead. In [5] it has been shown that this does not diminish the security of PACE as a password-based key-exchange protocol (as expressed in [6]), but rather adds strong impersonation resistance against active attacks excluding basically only man-in-the-middle attacks of the pure relaying type.

Subsequently, the German Federal Office for Information Security proposed a yet more simplified version of the PACE|AA protocol [4], which was also independently suggested by Hanzlik et al. [11] and called SPACE|AA there. In their protocol, the card only needs to perform a modular division to authenticate (e.g., the hashing and the modular addition as in the Schnorr case for PACE|AA disappears). Hanzlik et al. also proposed a so-called leakage-resilient version where they change the original PACE protocol slightly, such that the card needs to perform an additional modular multiplication during the PACE steps, but can later authenticate without performing an additional operation. The drawback of this protocol is that it interferes with the PACE step and thus makes the derived protocol incompatible with the ICAO standards.

While the simplified PACE|AA proposals by [4] and by Hanzlik et al. [11] improve over the [5] suggestions in terms of efficiency, they nonetheless currently come with seemingly weaker security guarantees. That is, the presentation in [4] has not been accompanied by a cryptographic analysis. The authors in [11] define

Protocol	efficiency	adversary	remark
PACE|AA [5]	HASH, 1 MUL, 1 SUB	active	
SPACE|AA [4, 11]	1 DIV	passive	
leakage-res. SPACE|AA [11]	1 MUL	passive	modifies PACE
additive PACE|CA (here)	1 SUB	active	
multiplicative PACE|CA (here)	1 DIV	active	=SPACE|AA

Fig. 2. Overview over different protocols combining PACE with card authentication. Efficiency refers to the additional operations for the card to perform authentication (HASH=hash computation, MUL=multiplication over $\mathbb{Z}_q$, DIV=division over $\mathbb{Z}_q$, SUB=subtraction over $\mathbb{Z}_q$). Adversary type refers to impersonation resistance for the authentication step. Note that the table does *not* take the underlying cryptographic assumptions into account.

several security notions similar to standard notion of key secrecy for password-based schemes [3] and for impersonation resistance as in [5]. Unfortunately, they do not relate their notions to these standard definitions. Moreover, consulting the security proof reveals that they more or less only consider security against passive (i.e., eavesdropping) adversaries: in the proofs they rely on a simulator which is able to generate transcripts of communication for *honest* parties and use the simulator to show that their security notions are met. We remark that achieving passive security is often much easier than dealing with active adversaries. As an example, note that the (plain) PACE protocol, despite being password-based, provides strong cryptographic security under the Diffie-Hellman assumption *against passive adversaries.*

For an overview over the known protocols and their main characteristic see the upper part of the table in Figure 2.

1.2 Authentication with Strong Cryptographic Guarantees

Here we show that we can achieve the best of both worlds: a combination of PACE with authentication which essentially guarantees impersonation resistance for free, with efficiency even beyond the solution in [4, 11], and still achieving security against active adversaries. In our protocol PACE|CA (CA for chip authentication) the card needs to perform an additional modular subtraction to authenticate, without changing the "core" PACE protocol. Our solution comes at a small price, though. We rely on the knowledge-of-exponent assumption (to be precise, KEA1 [2, 10]) which says that one needs to know the discrete logarithm of one of the two values X, Y in order to compute the DH key of X and Y. Due to the structure of the PACE protocol we also need to introduce a related variant, called knowledge-of-base assumption (KBA), which says that if given X one can compute Y and the DH key of X and Y relative to some generator g, one must know g in order to do so. The KBA at first glance appears to be weaker than KEA1, but due to technical details this is not necessarily so. As a kind of sanity check we nonetheless show that KBA holds for generic algorithms.

As mentioned, in our PACE|CA protocol the card only needs to perform an additional modular subtraction to authenticate in a strong sense. In terms of performance this even outdoes the proposals in [4, 11] which require modular multiplications or divisions. Nonetheless, we can view the SPACE|AA proposal as a multiplicative version of our PACE|CA protocol where the card authenticates by an extra modular division (instead of a subtraction). By the similarity to the additive version we obtain a strong security proof for the multiplicative version against active adversaries as well, and therefore also this stronger security guarantee for the SPACE|AA protocol in [4, 11].

In summary, the (additive and multiplicative version of the) PACE|CA protocol neither conflicts with the description of the original PACE protocol nor its (password-based) security. At the same time it gives impersonation resistance for free, against active adversaries. Although this security proof requires somewhat strong assumptions, namely KEA1 and KBA, we emphasize that using this approach is advantageous over simply omitting authentication in the signature-based case because of the computational effort. Consult again Figure 2 for a comparison to the other protocols.

2   Security Model

As for the previous results for PACE we use the real-or-random security model for password-based key exchange protocols of Abdalla et al. [1] which extends the model of Bellare et al. [3]. We refer the reader to [5] for a comprehensive description, including some minor adaptations for covering long-term secrets as the card's signing key. Here we give a brief outline. The model for key secrecy also serves as a basis for the security model for impersonation resistance.

Key Secrecy. We consider security against active attacks in which the adversary has full control over the network. Basically, the adversary can send messages to honest parties via a Send command, also allowing for man-in-the-middle kind of attacks, and it receives the parties' answer immediately. The adversary can decide upon delivery of the reply to another honest party, again via the Send command. The adversary can also eavesdrop on executions between two honest parties via the Execute command which returns the transcript. The adversary has two further commands available, the Reveal and Test command. The first one, when called about a session of an honest user which has terminated and accepted, reveals the session key of that party. This models the leakage of the session keys. When testing a completed session of an honest party via the Test command, the adversary either gets the session key of that party, or receives random and independent session keys, the choice made according to a secret bit b. The adversary's goal is to tell the two cases apart and to predict b. If the adversary cannot distinguish the two cases this means that the genuine session key derived in that execution "looks random" and is secure.

In addition, the adversary can gain control over an honest party during the attack via the Corrupt query. If used, then the adversary obtains the secrets of an honest party. As in [5] we devide this query into a Corrupt.pw and a Corrupt.key query where the former reveals the password only, and the latter reveals the long-term key only (in case of a chip). In both cases, the other secret remains private. An honest party gets adversarially controlled if it does not have any secrets left (i.e., if the adversary issues both Corrupt query types for a chip, or the Corrupt.pw query for the terminal). The extra command Register allows the adversary to register a public key pk^* in the name of a new user (identity). The user is immediately considered to be adversarial controlled and the password of the user is revealed to (or even chosen by) the adversary.

To prevent trivial attacks we assume that tested sessions are still *fresh* in the sense that, at the end of the attack, if there has been no Reveal query at any point to this session, neither has there been a Reveal query to a partner to U_i (to be defined next), nor has somebody been corrupted (i.e., neither kind of Corrupt query has been issued). Put differently, fresh sessions require that the session key has not been leaked (by neither partner) and that no Corrupt-query took place. Here, two sessions are partnered if both have terminated in accepting state with the same session identifies *sid* and the same partner identifier *pid*. Both values are defined by the protocol and the former should be basically some quasi unique information about the session, typically (parts of) the communication transcript, and the partner id should identify the intended partner.

We say that an adversary $\mathcal{A}$, running in time t (including the steps of the honest parties) and initiating at most q_e sessions and making at most q_h queries to the random oracle, *wins* if it predicts b correctly and all the instances in the Test queries have been fresh. Define the AKE advantage of an adversary $\mathcal{A}$ against the key agreement protocol P by

$$\mathbf{Adv}_P^{ake}(\mathcal{A}) := 2 \cdot \mathrm{Prob}[\mathcal{A} \text{ wins}] - 1$$

$$\mathbf{Adv}_P^{ake}(t, Q) := \max \left\{ \mathbf{Adv}_P^{ake}(\mathcal{A}) \ \middle| \ \mathcal{A} \text{ is } (t, Q)\text{-bounded for } Q = (q_e, q_h) \right\}$$

We note that PACE also achieves the notion of forward secrecy which basically says that it should not help the adversary if it corrupts some party after the Test query, and that even if corruptions take place before Test queries, then executions between honest users are still secure (before or after a Test-query). The advantage here is defined analogously and denoted by $\mathbf{Adv}_P^{ake-fs}(t, Q)$.

Impersonation Resistance. This security property says that the adversary, in the above attack, *successfully impersonates* if an honest reader in some session accepts with partner identity *pid* and session id *sid*, but such that (a) the intended partner U in *pid* is not adversarially controlled or the public key in *pid* has not been registered, and (b) no Corrupt.key command to U has been issued before the reader has accepted, and (c) the intended partner U does not successfully complete another session while session *sid* is running. This roughly means that the adversary managed to impersonate an honest chip or to make the reader accept a fake certificate, without knowing the long-term secret or relaying the data in a trivial man-in-the-middle kind of attack.

We note that requirement (c) is slightly stronger here than in the case of PACE|AA [5]. There, it is only demanded that the session id *sid* has not appeared in another accepting session. Here, we rather need to take into account the point in time in which this value *sid* could have been generated.

Define now the IKE advantage (I for impersonation) of an adversary $\mathcal{A}$ for a key agreement protocol P by

$$\mathbf{Adv}_P^{ike}(\mathcal{A}) := \mathrm{Prob}[\mathcal{A} \text{ successfully impersonates}]$$

$$\mathbf{Adv}_P^{ike}(t, Q) := \max\left\{\mathbf{Adv}_P^{ike}(\mathcal{A}) \mid \mathcal{A} \text{ is } (t, Q)\text{-bounded}\right\}$$

Note that we do not need to define a forward secure version here.

3   The PACE|CA Protocol

3.1   Protocol Description: Additive Version

Figure 3 illustrates the (additive version of the) PACE|CA protocol. PACE is a password-based Diffie-Hellman key exchange protocol over an elliptic curve with parameters $\mathcal{G} = (a, b, p, q, g, k)$. It consists of a first Diffie-Hellman step (for values g, Y_A, Y_B) in which a nonce s is also shared, encrypted under the joint password. The nonce is mixed via g^s to the Diffie-Hellman key for Y_A, Y_B to derive a generator $\hat{g}$. This generator is used in a subsequent DH key exchange (for $\hat{g}, Y_A', Y_B'$) to derive another key K, and the parties finally use this key K to derive the session keys and to authenticate (some of) the transmitted values via deterministically computed MACs T_A, T_B.

In the combined protocol with card authentication, PACE|CA, after the completion of the PACE step the card then authenticates by intertwining its contribution y_A to the first DH key with its long-term secret x_A by a simple subtraction, $\sigma = y_A - x_A \bmod q$. It sends this value σ together with the certificate for the public key $X_A = g^{x_A}$ over the already established channel. Note that this part is the crucial difference to the previous proposal PACE|AA [5], where the card computed a Schnorr or DSA signature based on y_A, x_A, requiring hashing and modular multiplication and addition. In contrast, here we merely need a modular subtraction.

We note that there are different suggestions on how to implement the step to derive the generator $\hat{g}$. The DH step as above, sometimes called generic mapping, currently appears to be the most prominent instantiation. A few instantiations use the alternative hashing-into-the-curve mapping [7,9,13]. The intertwining of PACE with the certification as above, however, is only know to work with the DH-based generic mapping.

3.2   Protocol Description: Multiplicative Version

As explained in the introduction, both the German Federal Office for Information Security [4] and Hanzlik et al. proposed a multiplicative version of the above

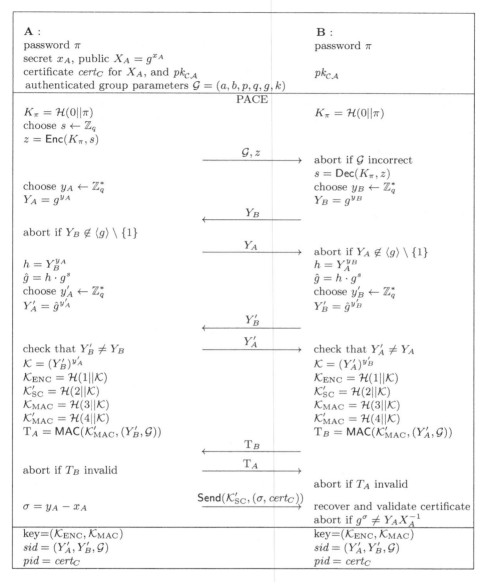

Fig. 3. The PACE|CA protocol (all operations are modulo q resp. over the curve)

protocol, which is identical to the additive one, except that the card finally transmits $\sigma = y_A \cdot x_A^{-1}$ and the reader checks that $X_A^\sigma = Y_A$. The full description is given in Appendix A.

4 Security Analysis

In our theorems we quantify the adversary's success probability in terms of the advantage against the deployed primitives, denoting in general by $\mathbf{Adv}_{\mathcal{S}}^{att}(t^*, Q)$ an upper bound on the success probability of any adversary against scheme $\mathcal{S}$, running in time at most t^* and making at most Q queries of the corresponding type. For secure channels, for example, we consider a simultaneous attack in which the adversary either tries to distinguish messages sent through the channel or to successfully inject or modify transmissions. We denote the adversary's advantage for an attack with u users and q challenge queries in this case by $\mathbf{Adv}_{SC}^{lor}(t^*, u, q)$. Formal definitions for all primitives can be found in Appendix B.

4.1 Key Secrecy

We first note that both the additive as well as the multiplicative PACE|CA protocol inherit their AKE security (i.e., key secrecy) from the original PACE protocol, just as in the case of PACE|AA [5]. That is,

Theorem 1. *The (additive and multiplicative) protocol PACE|CA satisfies:*

$$\mathbf{Adv}_{PACE|CA}^{ake}(t, Q) \leq \frac{q_e^2}{2q} + \mathbf{Adv}_{SC}^{lor}(t^*, q_e, q_e) + \mathbf{Adv}_{PACE}^{ake}(t^*, Q)$$

where $t^* = t + O(kq_e^2 + kq_h^2 + kq_{ic}^2 + k^2)$ and $Q = (q_e, q_{ic}, q_h)$, where q_e is the number of executions, q_{ic} the number of ideal cipher queries, and q_h is the number of random oracle queries.

The same argument holds in the forward-secure case.

The more intriguing proof is the one for impersonation resistance. In the PACE|AA case, with a Schnorr or DSA signature, i.e., where y_A was used as the randomness for creating the additional signatures, the security proof heavily relied on the chosen-message security of the underlying signature scheme. This basically allowed to create signatures for sessions in which the adversary communicated with an honest card. At the same time, when the adversary tried to impersonate as the card, one could extract a signature forgery. This option is not available anymore here, and hence we need a more sophisticated argument and somewhat stronger assumptions.

4.2 Assumptions for Impersonation Resistance

We use the standard notion of unforgeability for certificates, the success probability of any adversary running in time t^* and adaptively asking for at most q certificates denoted here as $\mathbf{Adv}_{\mathcal{CA}}^{forge}(t^*, q)$. We also use the common notion of MAC unforgeability, with the advantage of any adversary running in time t^* and making at most q_m MAC resp. q_v verification queries, denoted by $\mathbf{Adv}_{\mathcal{M}}^{forge}(t^*, q_m, q_v))$.

Another assumption we need is about the hardness of finding collisions in the (deterministic) MAC. That is, we denote by $\mathbf{Adv}_{\mathcal{M}}^{coll}(t^*)$ the probability of any algorithm running in time t^* to output a message m and a key k such that for a random key k', sampled afterwards, it happens that $\mathsf{MAC}(k, m) = \mathsf{MAC}(k', m)$. We evaluate this assumption in more detail in Section 5.

Knowledge-of-Exponent Assumption. Besides these definitions we use the following KEA1 (knowledge of exponent) assumption [2, 10] in its basic version. This assumption roughly says that, if one can compute a Diffie-Hellman key then one already knows the discrete logarithm of one of the two values.

Definition 1 (KEA1). *The (t, t', ϵ)-KEA1 assumption holds if for any adversary $\mathcal{B}$ running in time t there exists an adversary $\mathcal{B}'$ running in time t' such that the following experiment has probability at most ϵ to return 1 for any $(\mathcal{G}, g)$:*

> *pick $y \leftarrow \mathbb{Z}_q$ and compute $Y = g^y$*
> *let $(Z, K) \leftarrow \mathcal{B}(\mathcal{G}, g, Y)$*
> *let $z \leftarrow \mathcal{B}'(\mathcal{G}, g, Y)$*
> *return 1 iff $K = DH_g(Y, Z)$ but $K \neq Y^z$.*

We let $\mathbf{Adv}^{KEA1}(t, t')$ denote a (bound on the) value ϵ for which the KEA1 assumption holds for (t, t', ϵ).

Knowledge-of-Base Assumption. Unfortunately, the KEA1 assumption alone does not suffice in our setting. We need a somewhat "dual" assumption which says that, if one can complement a generator G and random group element Y by pair (Z, K) to a DH tuple then one already knows the base G. Put differently, the only way to compute the DH key K is by raising G to the z-th power, thus knowing $z = \log_G Z$ and therefore also $G = Z^{1/z}$, and then computing $K = Y^z$. In other words, one cannot ignore G and not rely on knowledge about it. In this sense, our KBA (knowledge-of-base assumption) is somewhat weaker than KEA1 (also, because one does not need to compute the discrete logarithm z but only a group element). On the other hand, we require that one can compute G from the Diffie-Hellman tuple (Y, Z, K) only, i.e., not receiving G as input, making the assumption somewhat stronger than KEA1 where the generator is given as input. In any case, our KBA seems to be close in spirit to KEA1 in the sense that both say that one needs to know how Z was generated.

In the definition below we need to exclude $z = 0$ and $Z = 1$, or else G would not be uniquely determined. Indeed, if $Z = 1$ then the tuple $(Y, 1, 1)$ would then information-theoretically hide G. The same is true for $Y = 1$. Indeed, when considering two bases G, G' and $Y = G^y, Z = G^z$ and $K = G^{yz} = (G')^{yz \log_{G'} G}$, we have $DH_{G'}(Y, Z) = (G')^{yz \log_{G'}^2 G}$. For $y, z \neq 0$ these two values can only be equal if $\log_{G'} G = 0$ or $\log_{G'} G = 1$. In the latter case the two elements G, G' are equal, and in the former case $G = 1$ which cannot happen for $Y, Z \neq 1$.

Definition 2 (KBA). *The (t, t', ϵ)-KBA holds if for any adversary $\mathcal{B}$ running in time t there exists an adversary $\mathcal{B}'$ running in time t' such that the following experiment has probability at most ϵ to return 1 for any $(\mathcal{G}, g)$ and any $G \in \langle g \rangle$:*

> *pick $y \leftarrow \mathbb{Z}_q$ and compute $Y = G^y$*
> *let $(Z, K) \leftarrow \mathcal{B}(\mathcal{G}, g, G, Y)$*
> *let $G' \leftarrow \mathcal{B}'(\mathcal{G}, g, Y, Z, K)$*
> *return 1 iff $Y, Z \neq 1$ and $K = DH_G(Y, Z)$, but $G \neq G'$.*

We let $\boldsymbol{Adv}^{KBA}(t, t')$ denote a (bound on the) value ϵ for which the KBA assumption holds for (t, t', ϵ).

We elaborate on the soundness of this assumption in Section 5.

4.3   Impersonation Resistance

We state security for both protocol versions simultaneously (as the claims are identical) but proof the additive version in full detail and then discuss that the same proof strategy applies to the multiplicative version, too:

Theorem 2 (Impersonation Resistance). *Both the additive and the multiplicative version of the protocol PACE| CA satisfy:*

$$\boldsymbol{Adv}_P^{ike}(t, Q) \leq \frac{q_e^2}{2q} + \boldsymbol{Adv}_{\mathcal{CA}}^{forge}(t, q_c) + q_e \cdot \boldsymbol{Adv}_{\mathcal{M}}^{forge}(t^*, 0) + q_h q_e \cdot \boldsymbol{Adv}_{\mathcal{M}}^{coll}(t^*)$$

$$q_c q_e \cdot \left(\boldsymbol{Adv}^{KEA1}(t, t^*) + \boldsymbol{Adv}^{KBA}(t, t^*) \right)$$

where $t^* = t + O(kq_e^2 + kq_h^2 + k^2)$ and $Q = (q_e, q_c, q_h)$, where q_e is the number of executions, q_c is the number of cards, and q_h is the number of random oracle queries.

Proof. Recall that we prove security of the additive version here. We first note that we can exclude the case that impersonation succeeds for a valid certificate for some key X which has not been certified by the $\mathcal{CA}$. This would straightforwardly contradict the unforgeability of the cerification scheme, noting that we can simulate $\mathcal{A}$'s attack when knowing the secret keys of the cards and following the prescribed protocol description for all honest parties (including the ability to decrypt the certificates in the final message of the impersonation attempts).

We continue to exclude further attack strategies of the adversary. First note that we can assume that all keys K computed in sessions by honest cards are distinct. This follows as Y_A' is chosen at random *after* the adversary has provided Y_B' and we check that $Y_B' \neq 1$. Then the key is a random group element and we therefore "lose" a collision probability of at most $\frac{1}{2q} q_e^2$ if we assume that no two keys in such executions are identical. Note that we cannot have the same key in the (fresh) impersonation attempt as in (at most) one of the other executions of the honest card, because for a fresh impersonation attempt the honest card cannot successfully complete an execution and compute such a key.

We next conclude that, most likely, the adversary, in an execution with an honest card, cannot send a valid MAC T_B without having queried the random oracle about the corresponding key K before. This follows from the (key-only) unforgeability of the MAC scheme: it would be straightforward to build a successful attacker against the MAC scheme, emulating the impersonation attack with the help of the secrets of all parties. Guess one of the executions with the honest cards and, when $\mathcal{A}$ sends T_B for $(Y'_A, \mathcal{G})$, output this pair as a forgery attempt. If the guess was correct then, since the key K is not used elsewhere, we can assume that the random oracle maps to the external (unknown) key $\mathcal{K}'_{\mathrm{MAC}}$ such that the pair constitutes a valid forgery. We lose a success probability of at most $q_e \cdot \mathbf{Adv}_{\mathcal{M}}^{forge}(t^*, 0)$.

We next show that in an execution with an honest card there cannot exist two MAC keys $\mathcal{K}'_{\mathrm{MAC}}$, returned as random oracle queries to the adversary, such that T_B verifies under both keys. Else it would be straightforward to contradict the collisions resistance of the MAC scheme. That is, we claim that the probability that for some T_B valid under $\mathcal{K}'_{\mathrm{MAC}}$ the probability that another randomly sampled key $\mathcal{K}''_{\mathrm{MAC}}$ in some other execution of the honest card also verifies T_B as valid, is bounded from above by $q_h q_e \cdot \mathbf{Adv}_{\mathcal{M}}^{coll}(t^*)$. To this end, simulate again the impersonation attack with all secrets and also pick one of the at most q_e executions with the honest card at random, and also one of the q_h hash queries the adversary makes. Wait for the adversary receive Y'_A in the predicted execution, before computing the MAC key, and output $m = (Y'_A, \mathcal{G})$ as the collision attempt together with the MAC key derived in the q_h-th hash query (if this hash query has not been made yet then pick a random key instead). Since all DH keys in executions with the honest card are distinct, any further key, also the one in the predicted execution, is independent and has not been queried before m is output. It follows that, if $\mathcal{A}$ accidentally finds $\mathcal{K}'_{\mathrm{MAC}}, \mathcal{K}''_{\mathrm{MAC}}$ and the value T_B computed from $\mathcal{K}'_{\mathrm{MAC}}, (Y'_A, \mathcal{G})$, we get a collision against the MAC scheme. Since we guess the right keys with probability $1/q_h q_e$ the claim follows.

Note that the former two restrictions say that the adversary queries the right DH key, and that this key is uniquely determined by the MAC in the execution via the hash queries.

We next note that we can restrict ourself to a single impersonation attempt; the case of more attempts can be reduced to the single-attempt case via guessing, losing a factor $1/q_e$ in the success probability. This is possible since we can easily simulate the terminal's side in the other attempts with the help of the public data. Similarly, we can also assume that there is only one honest card; else we again guess the right card which the adversary is going to attack in the single attempt (which is identified by the fact that the adversary only uses a certified public key). We again lose a factor of $1/q_c$ in the probability.

Computing Discrete Logarithms. Given an active attacker $\mathcal{A}$ on impersonation resistance, now in the presence of a single card and making only one impersonation attempt and with the further restrictions on successful attacks as above, we show how to construct a discrete-log finder $\mathcal{D}$ which on input $\mathcal{G}, g, X$ returns $x = \mathrm{DLOG}_g(X)$. Algorithm $\mathcal{D}$ operates as follows. It initializes the attack scenario for $\mathcal{A}$ with the data $\mathcal{G}, g$ as the system's parameters, and $X_A = X$ as the card's public key. It also plays the certification authority and creates the certificate for X. $\mathcal{D}$ also hands over the password of the card to the adversary immediately. It initially picks an index i between 1 and q_H, the number of $\mathcal{A}$'s hash queries, at random. Basically, this index i will be the guess for the hash query about the key computed in the impersonation attempt. In the course of the simulation we assume that $\mathcal{D}$ simulates the random oracle via lazy sampling, with one exception discussed below.

To simulate one of the concurrent interactions of the adversary $\mathcal{A}$ with the honest card, $\mathcal{D}$ proceeds as follows:

- Pick $s \leftarrow \mathbb{Z}_q$ as in the protocol and send $\mathcal{G}$ and $z = \mathsf{Enc}(K_\pi, s)$ on behalf of the card.
- Wait for the adversary $\mathcal{A}$ to send some Y_B (and check that Y_B is well-formed; abort if not).
- Pick $y_A \leftarrow \mathbb{Z}_q$ but now compute and send $Y_A = g^{y_A} \cdot X$. (In the unlikely case that $Y_A = 1$ we have already found $\mathrm{DLOG}_g X = y_A$ and can abort; we assume for simplicity therefore that $Y_A \neq 1$ is well formed.)
- Wait for the adversary to send Y_B' (and check its correctness).
- Pick a random $\tilde{y_A}' \leftarrow \mathbb{Z}_q$ and compute $Y_A' = g^{\tilde{y_A}'}$.
- Wait for the adversary to send T_B. Search through all hash queries of $\mathcal{A}$ for a query $4\|K$ such that T_B verifies for the answer $\mathcal{K}'_{\mathrm{MAC}}$. If there is no such key, abort this execution. If there are two or more such keys, then abort the whole simulation with an error message. Else, we may assume that K is the DH key to Y_A' and Y_B', and $\mathcal{D}$ can complete the simulation by using the key K and following the card's strategy, except when computing $y_A - x_A$; instead use the value y_A directly (without subtracting x_A).

It is easy to see that, if $\mathcal{D}$ uses the right key K —which it does according to the fact that the adversary must have queried about the key and that this key for which verification succeeds is unique— then the distribution of the simulated data is identical to the one of the actual card.

Now suppose $\mathcal{A}$ makes the impersonation attempt. Then $\mathcal{D}$ emulates the terminal's side in the attempt as follows:

- Initially, $\mathcal{A}$ sends some $\mathcal{G}, z$ on behalf of the honest card. Act like the honest terminal with the help of the password to decrypt z to s and to check the validity of $\mathcal{G}$.
- Pick a random Y_B and send it to the adversary.
- Upon receiving Y_A and checking that $Y_A \neq 1$, reply with a random Y_B'.
- When receiving Y_A' we let $\mathcal{D}$ check whether the i-th query of $\mathcal{A}$ to the random oracle has already been made or not. If so, then we take the corresponding key K from the query and ask our own simulated random oracle about $4\|K$ to derive the MAC key $\mathcal{K}'_{\mathrm{MAC}}$. Else we pick a fresh key $\mathcal{K}'_{\mathrm{MAC}}$ for this at random (and will later supply these keys as responses in the i-th query and all subsequent queries about the same input key $4\|K$). Faithfully compute the MAC with the help of this session key $\mathcal{K}'_{\mathrm{MAC}}$ and send the MAC T_B to the adversary.
- Upon receiving a MAC T_A from the adversary, together with the final encrypted value w, verify the correctness of the MAC and check and decrypt to recover w with the corresponding keys derived from K. Verify that $g^w = Y_A X^{-1}$.

Assume for the moment that $\mathcal{D}$ does not abort, that $\mathcal{A}$ at some point queries the random oracle about the Diffie-Hellman key K in the impersonation attempt, and that $\mathcal{D}$ correctly guesses the right query. Then, according to the KEA1 assumption, we can view the combined $\mathcal{A}$-$\mathcal{D}$ execution as an algorithm $\mathcal{B}$ which receives $\mathcal{G}, g$ and Y'_B as a power for some $G = \hat{g}$ (possibly unknown to us) as input and outputs (Y'_A, K) where, assuming a good guess for the hash query, K is the Diffie-Hellman key of Y'_A, Y'_B relative to $G = \hat{g}$. By the KBA there exists then an algorithm $\mathcal{B}'$ which, when run on input $(\mathcal{G}, g, Y'_B, Y'_A, K)$, returns $G = \hat{g}$, except with some small error probability.

Analogously, we can imagine that we view Y_A and $\hat{g}g^{-s}$ as a Diffie-Hellman completion for g, Y_B. Hence, by KEA1 and if we view the joint execution of $\mathcal{A}$-$\mathcal{D}$ and the KBA algorithm $\mathcal{B}'$ as an algorithm $\mathcal{B}$, we can conclude that there exists a KEA1 algorithm $\mathcal{B}''$ which, on input $(\mathcal{G}, g, Y_B)$ outputs $y_A = \log_g Y_A$ with roughly the same probability. But then we have

$$x = \log_g X = \log_g X_A = y_A - w.$$

We can thus compute the discrete logarithm of X.

Analysis. Note that $\mathcal{D}$ perfectly simulates the environment of $\mathcal{A}$'s attack (with all stipulations) if it predicts the i-th random oracle correctly. Since up the point where the query is made the simulation is perfectly indistinguishable it follows that the probability of a good guess is at least $1/q_h$. Conditioning on this, $\mathcal{D}$ perfectly simulates a random oracle and gets a valid output from $\mathcal{A}$ (under the restrictions). Running the KBA and KEA1 algorithms then yields the discrete logarithm with high probability. □

Note that the same proof strategy above applies to the multiplicative version as well. Basically, to simulate a communication with the honest card for the multiplicative version, algorithm $\mathcal{D}$ generates Y_A now as $Y_A = X_A^{y_A}$ (instead of $Y_A = g^{y_A} \cdot X_A$ as in the additive case) such that it can later provide y_A directly as σ. Vice versa, algorithm $\mathcal{D}$ eventually receives w from the impersonation attempt and checks that $X_A^w = Y_A$ (instead of $g^w = Y_A X_A^{-1}$). By the KEA1 and KBA assumptions, algorithm $\mathcal{D}$ obtains $y_A = \log_g Y_A$, too, such that $x = \log_g X = y_A \cdot w^{-1} \bmod q$. Here we can assume that $w \neq 0$ because of the verifications $X_A^w = Y_A$ and $Y_A \neq 1$.

5   Security Considerations

5.1   On the Generic Hardness of KBA

Note that, unlike the KEA1 problem which has been investigated before in [2,10], the KBA problem is new. To support the correctness of the assumption we discuss that the KBA problem is hard for generic algorithms, i.e., algorithms which do not exploit special properties of underlying group except for performing basic operations. More precisely, we work in Shoup's model [14] where the algorithm

$\mathcal{B}$ receives as input group elements g, G, Y (with logarithms $\delta = \log_g G \neq 0$ and $\gamma = \log_g Y \neq 0$ because $G, Y \neq 1$) and can "only" compute any $linear$ polynomial P in δ, γ. These polynomials represent the exponents of the derivable group elements, created by multiplication of group elements and exponentiation with constants (corresponding to additions of variables and multiplications with scalars in the exponent). In particular, the output values Z, K of algorithm $\mathcal{B}$ must be representable as polynomials

$$P_Z(\delta, \gamma) = a + b\delta + c\gamma \quad \text{for } Z$$

for known $a, b, c \in \mathbb{Z}_q$, and,

$$P_K(\delta, \gamma) = d + e\delta + f\gamma \quad \text{for } K$$

for known $d, e, f \in \mathbb{Z}_q$. For a successful run, we must have that K matches the Diffie-Hellman key of Y and Z relative to G, i.e., the value Z raised to the power γ/δ. As a polynomial, P_K must match

$$P_{DH}(\delta, \gamma) = a\gamma/\delta + b\gamma + c\gamma^2/\delta$$

and we must thus have that

$$\Delta(\delta, \gamma) = P_{DH}(\delta, \gamma) - P_K(\delta, \gamma) = a\gamma/\delta + (b - f)\gamma + c\gamma^2/\delta - e\delta - d.$$

is 0. Note that this polynomial can only be the zero-polynomial if $a = c = e = d = 0$ and $b = f$. In this case we have that $Z = G^b$ for a known b such that we can have algorithm $\mathcal{B}'$ simply output $Z^{1/b}$, where we use the fact that $b \neq 0$, or else for $a = b = c = 0$ the value Z would be 1 which is not an admissible output.

Finally, assume that Δ is not the zero-polynomial. It is then of degree at most 3 in the unknowns γ and $1/\delta$ (where we can substitute $1/\delta$ by $\delta' = 1/\delta$). Then, according to Shoup's result the probability that this polynomial vanishes, if $\mathcal{B}$ makes at most m group operations, is at most $O((3m + m^2)/q)$. This also takes into account the collision probability $O(m^2/q)$ It follows that $\mathcal{B}'$ finds the generator G by using b, except with probability ϵ at most $O((3t + t^2)/q)$, and within the same number of steps (plus the time to compute the inverse to b and raising Z to this power).

5.2   On the Necessity of KEA1 and KBA

Note that we show the KEA1 and KBA assumptions to be sufficient to prove PACE|CA to be secure. Still, we remark that it is currently unclear if they are also necessary. Suppose for example that an adversary would be able to refute the KEA1 assumption, i.e., would be able to compute DH keys without knowing the discrete logarithm of one of the values explicitly. Then we are not aware how this fact could be used to effectively attack the protocol. Indeed, the signature value $\sigma = y_A - x_A$ would still not necessarily leak the card's secret key x_A, because the blinding term y_A is not revealed in clear (but still used to compute a DH key).

5.3   On the Collision Resistance of the MAC

We briefly discuss the collision resistance property of the suggested MACs for PACE [8] for the terminal's authentication token. PACE suggests to use either an AES-based CMAC according to NIST 800-38b, or a 3DES retail mode MAC according to ISO/IEC 9797-1 (algorithm 3, padding method 2 with block cipher DES, and IV = 0.) Note that both MAC algorithms are deterministic such that a MAC value is uniquely determined given the key k and the message m.

First note that CMAC, in the final step, adds a (sub)key k_1 or k_2 before entering the final block cipher evaluation, depending on whether the padded message is aligned to block length or not. Assuming for simplicity that these subkeys are truly random (instead of pseudorandom) it follows that for a fixed message m the final block cipher invocation under independent main keys k, k' are also independent, the strength of the block cipher is irrelevant in this case. It follows that the probability that the MACs for such keys coincide, is $2^{-\text{output length}}$. Here it must be said, though, that PACE truncates the MAC to 8 bytes, such that we achieve a security level of 2^{-64} in this case (minus the amount for using pseudorandom subkeys). Still, note that this term is multiplied with $q_h q_e$ in our impersonation resistance theorem.

In the 3DES case the padded message is processed in CBC mode for key k_1, but in an additional final step one first decrypts the CBC value with another key k_2 first, before encrypting under k_1 again. This implies that, once m is fixed, assuming that the block cipher is (pseudo)random and that the subkey k_2 is independent of k_1, the probability of hitting a collision is again at most $2^{-\text{output length}}$. Since the output size is already 8 bytes we again achieve a bound of 2^{-64} (minus the amount for the "pseudorandomness assumptions")

We note that finding a collision in the MACs is not known to yield an immediate attack. We show that ruling them out is sufficient to make our simulation go through; it is open if this assumption is also necessary. In fact, our results show that the adversary must have queried the hash oracle about the correct key before sending T_B such that it (implicitly) knows the correct key; it may not explicitly know which of the evaluations yielded the correct key, though. Indeed, the adversary may try to learn itself the correct key only through the card's resp. simulator's reply. We are not aware how one can take advantage of such a behavior. If we assume that the attacker is well aware of the correct key (and we can formally forward these information to the simulator) then this collision probability disappears from the security bound.

Acknowledgments. We thank the anonymous reviewers of InTrust 2013 for helpful comments.

References

1. Abdalla, M., Fouque, P.-A., Pointcheval, D.: Password-based authenticated key exchange in the three-party setting. In: Vaudenay, S. (ed.) PKC 2005. LNCS, vol. 3386, pp. 65–84. Springer, Heidelberg (2005)

2. Bellare, M., Palacio, A.: The knowledge-of-exponent assumptions and 3-round zero-knowledge protocols. In: Franklin, M. (ed.) CRYPTO 2004. LNCS, vol. 3152, pp. 273–289. Springer, Heidelberg (2004)
3. Bellare, M., Pointcheval, D., Rogaway, P.: Authenticated key exchange secure against dictionary attacks. In: Preneel, B. (ed.) EUROCRYPT 2000. LNCS, vol. 1807, pp. 139–155. Springer, Heidelberg (2000)
4. Bender, J.: Chip authentication for ICAO. ISO/IEC JTC1 SC17 WG3 Meeting (March 2012)
5. Bender, J., Dagdelen, Ö., Fischlin, M., Kügler, D.: The PACE|AA protocol for machine readable travel documents, and its security. In: Keromytis, A.D. (ed.) FC 2012. LNCS, vol. 7397, pp. 344–358. Springer, Heidelberg (2012)
6. Bender, J., Fischlin, M., Kügler, D.: Security analysis of the PACE key-agreement protocol. In: Samarati, P., Yung, M., Martinelli, F., Ardagna, C.A. (eds.) ISC 2009. LNCS, vol. 5735, pp. 33–48. Springer, Heidelberg (2009)
7. Brier, E., Coron, J.-S., Icart, T., Madore, D., Randriam, H., Tibouchi, M.: Efficient indifferentiable hashing into ordinary elliptic curves. In: Rabin, T. (ed.) CRYPTO 2010. LNCS, vol. 6223, pp. 237–254. Springer, Heidelberg (2010)
8. BSI: Advanced security mechanism for machine readable travel documents extended access control (EAC). Tech. Rep (BSI-TR-03110) Version 2.05 Release Candidate, Bundesamt fuer Sicherheit in der Informationstechnik, BSI (2010)
9. Coron, J.-S., Gouget, A., Icart, T., Paillier, P.: Supplemental access control (PACE v2): Security analysis of PACE integrated mapping. In: Naccache, D. (ed.) Cryphtography and Security: From Theory to Applications. LNCS, vol. 6805, pp. 207–232. Springer, Heidelberg (2012)
10. Hada, S., Tanaka, T.: On the existence of 3-round zero-knowledge protocols. In: Krawczyk, H. (ed.) CRYPTO 1998. LNCS, vol. 1462, pp. 408–423. Springer, Heidelberg (1998)
11. Hanzlik, L., Krzywiecki, Ł., Kutyłowski, M.: Simplified PACE|AA protocol. In: Deng, R.H., Feng, T. (eds.) ISPEC 2013. LNCS, vol. 7863, pp. 218–232. Springer, Heidelberg (2013)
12. ICAO: Machine readable travel documents. Tech. Rep. Doc 9303, Part 1 Machine Readable Passports, 6th edn., International Civil Aviation Organization, ICAO (2006)
13. Icart, T.: How to hash into elliptic curves. In: Halevi, S. (ed.) CRYPTO 2009. LNCS, vol. 5677, pp. 303–316. Springer, Heidelberg (2009)
14. Shoup, V.: Lower bounds for discrete logarithms and related problems. In: Fumy, W. (ed.) EUROCRYPT 1997. LNCS, vol. 1233, pp. 256–266. Springer, Heidelberg (1997)

A   Multiplicative Version of PACE|CA

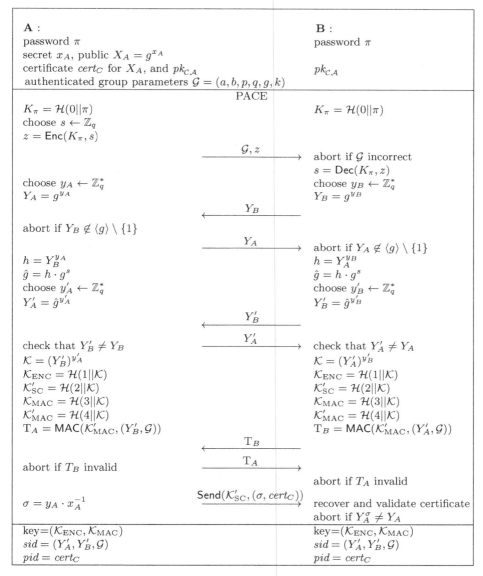

Fig. 4. The multiplicative PACE|CA protocol (all operations are modulo q resp. over the curve)

B   Definitions

This part of the paper here is almost verbatim from the full version of [5].

Message Authentication Codes. A message authentication code $\mathcal{M}$ consists of three efficient algorithms (KGen, MAC, Vf) where we assume again that keys are just random strings in the range of the hash function —making KGen obsolete— and that $MAC(k, m)$ maps any message to a MAC (resp. tag) T which is verifiable with the help of $Vf(k, m, T)$ with binary output. Completeness demands again that for any key k and any message m the value $T \leftarrow MAC(k, m)$ makes $Vf(k, m, T)$ return 1.

We require that the message authentication code $\mathcal{M}$ is unforgeable under adaptively chosen-message attacks. That is, the adversary is granted oracle access to $MAC(k, \cdot)$ and $Vf(k, \cdot, \cdot)$ for random key k and wins if it, at some point, makes a verification query (m, T) about a message m which has not been sent previously to MAC, and such that Vf returns 1 for this message. We denote by $\mathbf{Adv}_{\mathcal{M}}^{forge}(t, q_m, q_v)$ a (bound on the) value ϵ for which no attacker in time t can win (making at most q_m MACs queries and q_v verification queries) with probability more than ϵ.

Signatures and Certificates. A signature scheme $\mathcal{S} = $ (SKGen, Sig, SVf) consists of efficient algorithms for creating key pairs (sk, pk), signing messages $s \leftarrow Sig(sk, m)$, and verifying signatures, $d \leftarrow SVf(pk, m, s)$ with $d \in \{0, 1\}$. It must be that for signatures created under valid key pairs SVf always returns 1 (correctness). Unforgeability says that no algorithm should be able to forge the signer's signature. That is, a signature scheme $\mathcal{S} = $ (SKGen, Sig, SVf) is (t, q_s, ϵ)-unforgeable if for any algorithm $\mathcal{A}$ running in time t the probability that $\mathcal{A}$ outputs a signature to a fresh message under a public key is $\mathbf{Adv}_{\mathcal{S}}^{forge}(t, q_s)$ (which should be negligible small) while $\mathcal{A}$ has access (at most q_s times) to a singing oracle. We note that for Schnorr signatures and DSA signatures, we actually need a stronger notion discussed in the next section.

We also assume a certification authority $\mathcal{CA}$, modeled like the signature scheme through algorithms $\mathcal{CA} = $ (CKGen, Certify, CVf), but where we call the "signing" algorithm Certify. This is in order to indicate that certification may be done by other means than signatures. We assume that the keys $(sk_{\mathcal{CA}}, pk_{\mathcal{CA}})$ of the $\mathcal{CA}$ are generated at the outset and that $pk_{\mathcal{CA}}$ is distributed securely to all parties (including the adversary). We also often assume that the certified data is part of the certificate. We define unforgeability for a certification scheme $\mathcal{CA}$ analogously to signatures, and denote the advantage bound of outputting a certificate of a new value in time t after seeing q_c certificates by $\mathbf{Adv}_{\mathcal{CA}}^{forge}(t, q_c)$. We assume that the certification authority only issues unique certificates in the sense that for distinct parties the certificates are also distinct; we besides assume that the authority checks whether the keys are well-formed group elements and that certificates are of a fixed length (depending on the security parameter only).

Secure Channel. A secure channel $\mathcal{SC} = $ (KGen, Send, Rec) consists of algorithms for generating keys KGen (we assume in this paper that the keys are random strings and that the hash function $\mathcal{H}$ maps to such strings), a sending algorithm $\mathsf{Send}(k, m)$ wrapping the message usually in an encrypted and authenticated container C, and a recover algorithm $\mathsf{Rec}(k, C)$ which on input a key k and a container C returns a message m or an error symbol $\perp$. We assume the usual notion of completeness that any faithfully wrapped message under any key is recovered through the recover algorithms. Roughly, we demand that a secure channel hides messages (as encryption schemes) but at the same time also provides authenticity of the sent messages (as in MAC schemes). Below we cover both notions in a single security experiment.

As for security of the secure channel, we consider left-or-right security in the multi-user setting. That is, we assume that u users pick random keys $k_1, k_2, \ldots, k_u$ and that a secret challenge bit $b \leftarrow \{0, 1\}$ is chosen. The adversary $\mathcal{A}$ gets no input and can then access a sending oracle $\mathcal{O}_{\mathsf{Send}}(b, k_1, \ldots, k_u, \cdot, \cdot, \cdot)$ which for triples (i, m_0, m_1) returns a container $\mathsf{Send}(k_i, m_b)$ of the left or right message under the i-th key. Here, we assume that $1 \leq i \leq u$ and that m_0 and m_1 are of equal length. In addition, the adversary can ask a recovering oracle $\mathcal{O}_{\mathsf{Rec}}(k_1, \ldots, k_u, \cdot, \cdot)$ about indices i and containers C of its choice, recovering either a message under key k_i or the error symbol. The adversary eventually outputs a guess $a \in \{0, 1\}$ for the challenge bit b. To measure simultaneously successful attacks against the authenticity property we set $a \leftarrow b$ if at some point during the attack the adversary manages to submit a container C to the recover oracle $\mathcal{O}_{\mathsf{Rec}}$ such that it receives $m \neq \perp$ and such that C has not been created by oracle $\mathcal{O}_{\mathsf{Send}}$ for the same user before.

Let $\mathbf{Adv}_{\mathcal{E}}^{lor}(\mathcal{A})$ be the probability that $a = b$ minus the pure guessing probability $1/2$, taking also into account the deliberate switch of a to b in case of successful attacks against the authenticity. Let $\mathbf{Adv}_{\mathcal{E}}^{lor}(t, u, q)$ be the maximal advantage for any adversary running in time t, with access to at most u users, and making in total q queries. We note that a standard hybrid argument shows that the advantage increases only by a factor u when moving to the single-user case, i.e., $\mathbf{Adv}_{\mathcal{E}}^{lor}(t, u, q) \leq u \cdot \mathbf{Adv}_{\mathcal{E}}^{lor}(t, 1, q)$. Hence, the common notion of security for symmetric schemes implies security in the multi-user setting (with a loss of a factor u).

A Spatial Majority Voting Technique to Reduce Error Rate of Physically Unclonable Functions

Patrick Koeberl, Jiangtao Li, and Wei Wu

Intel Labs, Intel Corporation
{patrick.koeberl,jiangtao.li,wei.a.wu}@intel.com

Abstract. The Physically Unclonable Function (PUF) is a promising hardware security primitive with a wide range of applications, such as secure key generation, device authentication, IP protection, and hardware entangled cryptography. Due to their physical construction, PUF responses are inherently noisy. Error correction codes can be used to turn noisy PUF responses into keys or static values for these applications. However, a general construction of error correction is expensive and could introduce high entropy loss for PUFs with high error rates. Some PUF pre-processing techniques have been proposed, such as temporal majority voting and dark bit schemes, applied before error correction. In this paper, we introduce a simple and yet effective method to reduce PUF error rate called Spatial Majority Voting (SMV). The idea is to group PUF bits together to produce a single, more stable bit from the group. Experimental data show that SMV works very well, reducing the mean error rate from 6.5% to 0.3% with a group size of 9 on SRAM PUFs implemented in 65 nm CMOS. We also show that SMV can be combined with the dark bits method to further reduce the error rate to less than 0.01%, thus avoiding the need for expensive error correction schemes.

1 Introduction

A Physically Unclonable Function (PUF) can be described as a physical system which when measured provides unique, unpredictable, and repeatable responses. Creating a physical copy of the PUF with an identical behavior is hard, thus resulting in a structure which is unclonable even by the manufacturer. Pappu introduced the PUF concept in his thesis [19]. In 2002, Gassend et al. introduced silicon PUFs in [6]. Silicon PUFs exploit the uncontrollable manufacturing variations which are a result of the integrated circuit fabrication process. Manufacturing variation of process parameters such as dopant concentrations and line widths manifest themselves as differences in timing behavior between physical instances of the same integrated circuit design.

Since the first development of silicon PUFs, a number of silicon PUF constructions have been proposed. Lee et al. [12] proposed the first arbiter PUF in 2004. Guajardo et al. [7] proposed the SRAM PUF in 2007. In 2008 Kumar et al. [11] introduced Butterfly PUFs and Maes et al. [17] proposed D type Flip-Flop PUFs. In 2012 Simons et al. [20] proposed Buskeeper PUFs. Note that

R. Bloem and P. Lipp (Eds.): INTRUST 2013, LNCS 8292, pp. 36–52, 2013.

SRAM PUFs, Butterfly PUFs, D type Flip-Flop PUFs, and Buskeeper PUFs are all memory based PUFs.

PUFs have become a promising security primitive with a wide range of applications. For example, PUFs are used for secure key generation in silicon [14,21,7,16], which eliminates the need for storing keys in non-volatile memory. It was stated in [18] that PUF based key generation provides advantages like physical unclonability and tamper evidence, compared to storing the keys in non-volatile memory. PUF has been proposed for online device authentication in a challenge-response authentication protocol [22] and for offline device authentication [10]. Recently, PUFs have been used in various hardware entangled cryptographic schemes and protocols, such as a PUF-based block cipher [1] and PUF-based oblivious transfer and key exchange protocols [4]. Many of these applications can be used for trusted computing or building trusted systems.

Since PUF responses are inherently noisy and may not be uniformly random, a post-processing algorithm is needed to convert noisy PUF responses into keys or static values in these applications. This process is known as the fuzzy extractor or helper data algorithm in the literature. Part of the fuzzy extractor is error correction. Several practical fuzzy extractor schemes [3,18] have been proposed for memory-based PUFs using various error correction codes, such as BCH, Reed-Muller, Golay codes, or repetition codes. It is easy to see that the higher error rate in the PUF response, the more error correction is required. Complex error correction codes are capable of correcting high error rates, but are much more expensive to build in hardware. Furthermore a general construction of error correction could introduce high entropy loss [5]. Therefore it is important to reduce the PUF bit error rate before applying the fuzzy extractor.

In this paper, we introduce a new technique to reduce the PUF error rate called Spatial Majority Voting (SMV). This technique is effective and simple to implement. The idea is to group a few PUF response bits together from which a subgroup is chosen. A more stable bit from the group is produced based on majority voting of the subgroup. Experimental data show SMV works well, reducing the mean error rate from 6.5% to 0.3% with a group size of 9 on SRAM PUFs implemented in 65 nm CMOS. Combining SMV with the dark bits method [1], the noisy rate in PUF can be reduced to less than 0.01%. A simple hardware implementation of Hamming codes, BCH codes (with small code size), or repetition codes can be used to remove the remaining PUF errors. Our solution opens a wide possibility of applications where expensive error correction codes are not possible, such as RFID and resource-constrained devices.

1.1   Related Work

There are techniques in the literature to reduce PUF noise rate before applying error correction or a fuzzy extractor to the PUF responses, namely, Temporal Majority Voting (TMV) [1], dark bits [1], and index based syndromes [23]. In this paper we term these methods pre-processing techniques and consider SMV similarly.

The basic idea of TMV [1] is as follows: each PUF bit is evaluated multiple times and if most of the time it is evaluated as 1, then we set this PUF bit value to 1; otherwise, we set this bit value to 0. Observe that if a PUF bit is relatively stable and only flips its value occasionally, TMV can effectively stabilize this bit. However, if a PUF bit is very unstable (e.g., probability of one half of being 0 and 1 respectively), TMV does not work well on this bit.

In the dark bits method presented by Armknecht et al. [1], each PUF bit is evaluated multiple times during the setup phase. If a PUF bit is not stable, we mark it as a "dark bit". In the evaluation phase, the PUF is evaluated again and the dark bits are discarded, as these bits were noisy during the setup phase. Observe that if a PUF bit is very unstable, it will very likely be detected as a dark bit. It is easy to see that filtering the PUF responses dark bits results in a lower error rate.

Yu and Devadas [23] provided a different technique called index based syndrome. This approach assumes the PUF output is a real value instead of a single bit. The idea is that only PUF bits with a strong representation of a "1" or a "0" are chosen. In other words, only relatively stable PUF bits are picked. This technique is only applicable to some PUF designs such as the Ring Oscillator PUF, but not applicable to memory-based PUFs with binary outputs.

Both TMV and the dark bits method require multiple PUF measurements which could be impractical in many applications according to [13]. The index based syndrome method only works for a few type of PUFs with real-valued output. In contrast, our SMV method does not require multiple PUF measurements and is applicable to all PUF types. Furthermore, the SMV method is complementary to these three techniques. We shall show in Section 5 that SMV can be combined with the dark bits method to further reduce PUF error rate significantly.

Another approach to reduce PUF error rate is to use a repetition code [3,18,2]. Using a repetition code of length n, a random bit b is repeated n times into an n-bit string and then XORed with an n-bit PUF response as the helper data. In the evaluation phase, the random bit b is recovered by XORing the helper data and the PUF response and then running a majority voting on the XORed result. Repetition codes are indeed more efficient than our SMV method in terms of PUF error rate reduction. However, there are two limitations to the repetition code method. First, repetition codes suffers high entropy loss. For an n-bit PUF response, the entropy loss is $n - 1$ and there is at most one bit of leftover entropy [5]. For low entropy PUFs, there could be zero leftover entropy using repetition coding. We believe there is less entropy loss in our SMV approach. Detailed analysis of entropy loss in SMV remains an open question and is future work. Second, the repetition code method can only be used in the code-offset construction (also known as fuzzy commitment [8] in the literature). In the application of PUF-based key generation using repetition codes, the key has to be chosen external to the device by a trusted manufacturer. In our SMV scheme, the key can be completely "unknown" to the manufacturer which is an attractive property for many applications.

1.2   Our Contributions

We summarize our contributions of this paper as follows: we provide an efficient pre-processing method to reduce PUF error rate using Spatial Majority Voting. Our SMV method is efficient to implement in hardware. We provide both theoretical analysis and experimental data to show that the SMV method works well. We note that if the raw PUF responses are biased, SMV would increase the bias in the processed PUF response. We provide an alternative SMV scheme such that the bias in PUF is not be amplified. We also present how to combine SMV with dark bits method such that the PUF error rate can be further reduced.

1.3   Organization of the Paper

The rest of this paper is organized as follows. We first introduce our SMV scheme in Section 2 with a theoretical analysis. We show the effectiveness of SMV with experimental studies on real SRAM PUF data in Section 3. We present an alternative SMV scheme for PUFs with biased responses in Section 4. In Section 5, we show that the SMV scheme can be combined with the dark bits method to further reduce the PUF error rate. We discuss the potential applications of our SMV scheme in Section 6 and conclude our paper in Section 7.

2   Basic Spatial Majority Voting Scheme

In this section, we first review a simplified PUF model and define the PUF pre-processing process. We then describe our Spatial Majority Voting (SMV) scheme and provide some theoretical analysis to show the effectiveness of SMV.

2.1   PUF Model and PUF Pre-processing Process

Roughly speaking, a PUF is a random function based on a physical system with a small amount of noise. Although there have been earlier attempts at formal definitions of PUF [19,6,7,1], we use a simplified PUF definition based on [1] with a focus on PUF stability. The other properties of PUF such as unclonablity, randomness, and tamper evidence are neglected from the following simplified model.

Definition 1 (Physically Unclonable Functions). *A (n, m, p_e)-family of physically unclonable functions is a set of probabilistic algorithms with the following procedures:*

Instantiate. *The output of the Instan procedure is a unique probabilistic function $f : \{0,1\}^n \to \{0,1\}^m$.*

Evaluate. *Given a physically unclonable function f, the Eval procedure on each challenge $x \in \{0,1\}^n$ outputs a noisy response $f(x) \in \{0,1\}^m$.*

On two separate evaluations of same f and challenge x, denoted as r_1 and r_2, the noise vector between two evaluations is $r_1 \oplus r_2$. The p_e is the average noise rate between any two PUF measurements.

Assuming the PUF noise is randomly distributed and is drawn independently for each bit of the PUF response, then the PUF noise rate p_e is also called the PUF bit error rate. In other words, the noise vector between two PUF measurements is a vector of m independent Bernoulli distributed random variables with probability p_e. This is commonly assumed in the PUF literature [7,1,9].

Katzenbeisser et al. [9] show that the average PUF bit error ranges from 2% to 30% for various silicon PUF constructions. As we discussed earlier, many applications of PUF require static PUF outputs. It is expensive to use general constructions of error correction or fuzzy extractors to reduce the PUF noise. We define the following "pre-processing" process to reduce PUF noise. The pre-processing process has two procedures: *setup* and *processing*. Let f be a physically unclonable function with parameters (n, m, p_e). The optional setup procedure outputs a helper data h, given f and a challenge x as input. The processing procedure outputs a pre-processed PUF response w, given f, x, and h as input.

Setup Procedure. On input of a PUF f and an n-bit challenge x, this procedure outputs a helper data h.

Processing Procedure. On input of a PUF f, a challenge x, and a helper data h, this procedure outputs pre-processed PUF response w.

In the setup or processing procedure, PUF may be evaluated once or multiple times. The goal of the pre-processing function is to reduce the noise in the "pre-processed" PUF responses for any given PUF f and challenge x, i.e., to reduce Hamming distance between two processed responses w and w'.

For example, Temporal Majority Voting (TMV) can be defined as follows. Let k be a small odd number and $t = (k+1)/2$ be the majority voting threshold. The TMV process has no setup procedure and has the following processing procedure.

TMV Processing. On input of a PUF f and a challenge x, f is evaluated k times and k responses obtained $w^{(1)}, \ldots, w^{(k)}$. Let $w_i^{(j)}$ be the i-th bit of $w^{(j)}$. This procedure outputs $w = w_1 \cdots w_m$, where $w_i = 1$ if $w_i^{(1)} + \cdots + w_i^{(k)} \geq t$ and $w_i = 0$ otherwise, for $i = 1, \ldots, m$.

Similarly the dark bits method can be defined as follows. Let k be a parameter for identifying dark bits. The idea of this method is to filter the noisy PUF bits that were observed during the setup procedure. These noisy PUF bits are recorded as a dark bits mask.

Dark Bits Setup. On input of a PUF f and a challenge x, f is evaluated k times and k responses obtained $w^{(1)}, \ldots, w^{(k)}$. Compute helper data $h = (w^{(1)} \oplus w^{(2)}) \vee \cdots \vee (w^{(1)} \oplus w^{(k)})$, where $\oplus$ is bitwise XOR and $\vee$ is bitwise OR. This h is called the dark bits mask.

Dark Bits Processing. On input of the PUF f, challenge x, and dark bits mask h. The processing procedure first evaluates f and obtains $\tilde{w}$, then discards the all bits marked in h from $\tilde{w}$, and produces a shorter output w.

2.2   Our SMV Scheme

In TMV, the PUF is measured multiple times and majority voting is applied on each bit location to filter the PUF noise. Inspired by TMV, we propose SMV in this section. The idea of SMV is to group a few PUF bits together to produce a more stable bit. A naïve method is to perform majority voting on the group, i.e., if there is more '1' in the group, set the group bit as 1, otherwise, set the group bit as 0. Unfortunately, this approach increases the PUF error rate as shown in Figure 1(right) instead of reducing the error rate. The analysis of the naïve SMV method is given in Appendix A.

The basic idea of our SMV scheme is that we divide PUF responses into groups and extract a stable bit from each group as follows: choose a majority subgroup from each group during the setup procedure, and then do majority voting on the subgroup. In the processing procedure, only the bits in subgroup are used for majority voting. Observe that all the bits in the subgroup have the same value in the setup procedure. If there is a small noise in the PUF response, e.g., only a small number of bits in the group flip, the majority voting would filter the noise.

We now formally describe the basic SMV method with the following parameters: k as the group size, k' as the subgroup size, and t as the voting threshold value. For our basic SMV scheme, we set $k = 2k' - 1$ and $k' = 2t + 1$. For example, $k = 9$, $k' = 5$, and $t = 2$.

SMV Setup. On input of a PUF f with parameters (n, m, p_e) and an n-bit challenge x, it runs the following steps:

1. Evaluate f on challenge x and obtains an m-bit PUF response w.
2. Divide w into l groups $G_1, \ldots, G_l$ of size k, where $l = \lfloor m/k \rfloor$.
3. For each group G_i, where $i = 1, \ldots, l$, do the following steps:
   (a) Let group bit b_i be the majority bit of the group G_i.
   (b) Let h_i be a k-bit mask that marks the majority subgroup, i.e., the location of first k' bits of b_i in G_i.
4. This function outputs the helper data $h = h_1, \ldots, h_l$.

SMV Processing. On input of the PUF f, challenge x, and helper data $h = h_1, \ldots, h_l$, it runs the following steps:

1. Evaluate f and obtains PUF response w.
2. Divide w into l groups $G_1, \ldots, G_l$ of size k, where $l = \lfloor m/k \rfloor$.
3. For each group G_i, where $i = 1, \ldots, l$, do the following steps:
   (a) Set t_i as the number of '1' in the subgroup of G_i marked by h_i.
   (b) Set the group bit $b_i = 1$ if $t_i > t$ and set $b_i = 0$ otherwise.
4. Output $b_1, \ldots, b_l$ as processed PUF response.

For example, if the PUF bits in a group G_i are read as $\{0,0,1,0,1\}$ during the setup procedure, the majority subgroup is the 1st, 2nd, and 4th bits of the group, and h_i is output as $\{1,1,0,1,0\}$. If PUF bits are read as $\{0,1,1,0,1\}$ in the processing procedure, the majority voting is conducted on $\{0,1,*,0,*\}$, where $*$ denotes the bits outside the voting subgroup. As a result, the group bit b_i is evaluated as 0.

We now calculate how SMV would reduce the PUF error rate. The raw PUF error rate is p_e. Observe that all the k' bits in the subgroup are the same during the setup procedure. The group bit in the setup procedure is the majority bit in the group. In the processing procedure, the group bit changes only if more than t bits in the subgroup flip their values during the PUF evaluation. Let us define binocdf as a binomial cumulative distribution function:

$$\text{binocdf}(t,n,p) = \sum_{i=0}^{t} \binom{n}{i} p^i (1-p)^{n-i}.$$

The error rate after SMV is then $1 - \text{binocdf}(t, k', p_e)$. We plot the error rate on the PUF response after SMV in Figure 1(left) and list a few error rate values in Table 1.

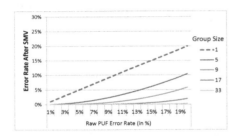
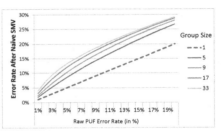

Fig. 1. Error rate reduction using our SMV (left) and naïve SMV (right)

Table 1. Estimated error rate after SMV with $k = 9, 13, 17$, respectively

Raw error rate	.01	.03	.05	.07	0.09	.11	.13	.15	.17
$k = 9$	.000010	.00026	.0012	.0031	.0063	.011	.018	.027	.037
$k = 13$	.000000	.000026	.00019	.00071	.0018	.0039	.0072	.012	.019
$k = 17$	.000000	.000003	.000033	.00017	.00055	.0014	.0030	.0056	.0098

Clearly, SMV is very effective even for a small group size, e.g., $k = 5$ or 9. It can quickly reduce the PUF error rate. Take $k = 9$ as example, if the raw PUF error rate is 15%, the error rate after SMV becomes 2.7% which is a 5x improvement. If the raw error rate is 5%, the error rate after SMV drops to 0.12% which is more than 40x improvement. As we shall see in Section 3, our theoretical analysis matches the SMV performance on real PUF data closely.

3 Experimental Result

We evaluate the performance of our SMV scheme using data collected from a silicon PUF implementation in 65 nm CMOS [15]. The dataset comprises 280 SRAM PUF measurements obtained across 96 device instances over a range of voltage supply and ambient temperature conditions. Table 2 tabulates the number of measurements collected at each operating condition.

Table 2. Number of test measurements recorded per device operating condition

	V=1.08V	V=1.2V	V=1.32V
T=25°C	30	60	30
T=+85°C	20	40	20
T=-40°C	20	40	20

The metrics of inter-distance and intra-distance are used as a measure of PUF performance both of the raw SRAM PUF and our SMV scheme. *Intra-distance* is a measure of the hamming distance between PUF responses taken from the same physical PUF instance. This metric is a measure of the PUF noise rate and should be as close as possible to zero. In the rest of this paper, we use the intra-distance μ_{intra} to refer the average PUF error rate in the PUF experimental data. *Inter-distance* measures the Hamming distance between two PUF responses taken from different physical PUF instances. The inter-distance metric is a measure of the uniqueness of a PUF response and ideally should be 50%.

Inter-distance and intra-distance results for the raw SRAM PUF on 96 devices using the operating conditions described above are shown in Figure 2. We chose an SRAM PUF size of 8704 bits, i.e., $m = 8704$. The results show near-ideal behavior with a mean fractional intra-distance of 6.5% and standard deviation of 0.010. The fractional intra-distance is 49.5% with a standard deviation of 0.006.

With the baseline performance of the raw SRAM PUF determined we now evaluate the performance of our SMV scheme for parameters of $l = 512$ and $k = 9, 13, 17$. Table 3 tabulates the results. In addition to the mean and standard deviation results for inter- and intra-distance we give the maximum intra-distance and mean bias in terms of ones in the SMV output. The intra-distance results show that SMV gives a significant reduction over the raw PUF noise rate, reducing the raw error rate from 6.5% to 0.31%, 0.09%, and 0.02%, respectively, with $k = 9$, 13, and 17. This aligns well with our theoretical analysis in Table 1, where if the raw PUF error rate is 7%, the error rate after SMV improves to 0.31%, 0.071%, and 0.017%, respectively, with $k = 9$, 13, and 17. Figure 3 shows the inter- and intra-distance results for the $k = 13$ and $k = 17$ case.

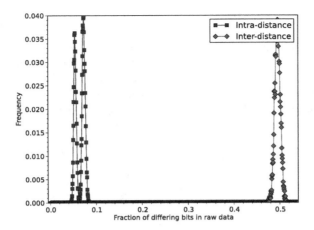

Fig. 2. Inter- vs intra-distances for raw SRAM PUF data (8704 bits)

Table 3. Experimental results before (raw PUF) and after SMV processing

	μ_{intra}	σ_{intra}	max_{intra}	μ_{inter}	σ_{inter}	$\mu_{bias(ones)}$
Raw PUF	.065119	.009900	.085133	.495468	.006009	.502098
SMV, $k=9$	.003080	.002653	.019531	.484900	.023696	.506249
SMV, $k=13$	.000852	.001350	.011718	.483650	.023797	.504457
SMV, $k=17$	.000241	.000691	.007812	.485729	.023695	.507814

4   Alternative SMV Scheme for Biased PUF Responses

Note that if the raw PUF responses are biased, then the bias will be amplified after SMV processing. For example, if the PUF response is biased toward 1, then it is more likely that the majority bit from the group has a similar bias. Let p_1 be the probability that a PUF bit response is 1. For our basic SMV scheme with parameters k, k', t,

$$\Pr\left[\text{group bit} = 1\right] = \Pr\left[\text{number of '1' bits in the group} \geq k'\right]$$
$$= 1 - \text{binocdf}(k' - 1, k, p_1)$$

Figure 4(left) shows that the bias rate quickly increases to 1 or decreases to 0 if the raw PUF bit is biased. This property makes our basic SMV scheme unusable for highly-biased PUFs, in particular for a large group size k. Studies have shown that [9] some PUF constructions (e.g., SRAM PUFs) are unbiased while other PUF constructions (e.g., Latch PUFs or Flip-Flop PUFs) exhibit a strong bias.

In this section, we provide an alternative SMV scheme for PUFs, such that SMV does not exacerbate an existing bias. The basic idea is as follows: let k be the group size, k' be the subgroup size, and t be the voting threshold value, where $k' = 2t + 1$. Instead of choosing $k = 2k' - 1$, choose a larger k, e.g., $k = 3k'$.

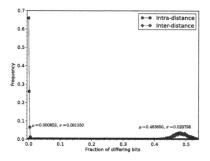 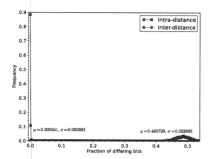

Fig. 3. Inter- vs intra-distances for SMV, k=13 (left) and k=17 (right)

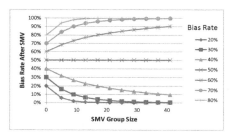 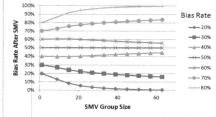

Fig. 4. Bias rate after basic SMV (left) and our alternative SMV (right)

During the setup procedure, for a group G_i, instead of setting the group bit as the majority bit, choose a random bit b_i as the group bit and choose the subgroup based on b_i. For cases where there are not enough b_i in the group, i.e., the number of b_i bits in the group is less than k', then we have to choose the opposite bit as the group bit. The processing procedure in the alternative SMV method is the same as the basic SMV method, i.e., conduct a majority voting on the subgroup. The alternative SMV setup procedure is as follows:

Alternative SMV Setup. On input of a PUF f and an n-bit challenge x, it
runs the following steps:
1. Evaluate f on challenge x and obtains an m-bit PUF response w.
2. Divide w into l groups $G_1, \ldots, G_l$ of size k, where $l = \lfloor m/k \rfloor$.
3. For each group G_i, where $i = 1, \ldots, l$, do the following steps:
   (a) Choose a random bit b_i.
   (b) If the number of b_i in G_i is less than k', set $b_i = 1 - b_i$.
   (c) Randomly choose k' number of b_i from G_i as the subgroup and use
       h_i to mask the subgroup location.
4. This function outputs the helper data $h = h_1, \ldots, h_l$.

In both basic SMV and alternative SMV, the majority voting is conducted on the subgroup. Therefore, the noise rate reduction depends on the subgroup size

k'. For the same k' value, the alternative SMV scheme requires a larger group size k, thus it is less efficient than the basic SMV. We now analyze the bias of the group bit. We use b to denote the group bit and b' to denote the random bit chosen in step 3(a) above. Let t_1 be the number of '1' bits in the group and t_0 be the number of '0' bits in the group.

$$\Pr[b = 1] = \Pr[b = 1 \vee b' = 1] \cdot \Pr[b' = 1] + \Pr[b = 1 \vee b' = 0] \cdot \Pr[b' = 0]$$
$$= 0.5 \cdot \Pr[t_1 \geq k'] + 0.5 \cdot \Pr[t_0 < k']$$
$$= 0.5(1 - \mathrm{binocdf}(k' - 1, k, p_1)) + 0.5(1 - \mathrm{binocdf}(k - k', k, p_1))$$

Figure 4(right) plots the bias rate of the group bit with respect to different bias rates in the raw PUF response and different group sizes. We use $k = 3k'$ and $k' = 3, 5, \ldots, 21$. Observe that if the bias rate in the raw PUF response is 60%, the bias rate after the alternative SMV decreases. However, if the raw PUF response is very biased, the bias rate in the group bit increases. This shows that the alternative SMV scheme is fairly effective for slightly biased PUF but less effective for highly biased PUF.

5   Combining SMV with the Dark Bits Method

We observe from Figure 1(left) that for a given group size SMV is more efficient at low raw error rates. In other words, SMV achieves a super-linear rather than linear error-rate reduction. Taking $k = 9$ as an example, Table 1 shows that if the raw PUF error rate is 15%, the error rate after SMV becomes 2.7% which is a 5x improvement. If the raw error rate is 5%, the error rate after SMV drops to 0.12% which is more than 40x improvement. The reduction ratio continues to increase with decreasing raw error rate. The same trend is observed analytically for other group sizes.

In order to exploit the efficiency of SMV at low raw error rates, we propose to combine SMV with other techniques, for example using a dark bit scheme. The dark bit method is a way to remove unstable PUF bits. More specifically, we run multiple PUF measurements during the setup procedure. If a PUF bit is noisy, we mark it as a dark bit and exclude it from further processing. The resultant dark bit mask is stored externally as part of the helper data. We apply the dark bit technique first and reduce the raw error rate to a reasonably low level. SMV is subsequently applied to further reduce the overall error rate.

A formal description of the dark bit augmented SMV method follows. It has the following two parameters o as the number of PUF measurements in the setup procedure and k as the SMV group size. We use DarkSMV(o, k) to denote this method with parameters o and k.

DarkSMV Setup. On input of a PUF f and a challenge x, f is obtained
1. f is evaluated o times and o responses obtained $w^{(1)}, \ldots, w^{(o)}$. Compute dark-bit mask $\mathrm{mask} = (w^{(1)} \oplus w^{(2)}) \vee \cdots \vee (w^{(1)} \oplus w^{(o)})$.
2. Divide $w^{(1)}$ into l groups $G_1, \ldots, G_l$ of size k, where $l = \lfloor m/k \rfloor$.

3. Divide mask into l groups of masks $mask_1, \ldots, mask_l$ of size k.
4. For each group G_i, where $i = 1, \ldots, l$, do the following steps:
   (a) Discard the dark bits in G_i using the dark bits mask $mask_i$.
   (b) Let group bit b_i be the majority bit of the group G_i, after the dark bits have been discarded. If there is a tie, choose b_i randomly.
   (c) Let h_i be a k-bit mask that marks the majority subgroup, i.e., the location of bits with value b_i in G_i without the dark bits.
5. This function outputs the helper data $h = h_1, \ldots, h_l$.

DarkSMV Processing. On input if the PUF f, challenge x, and and helper data $h = h_1, \ldots, h_l$.

1. Evaluate f and obtains PUF response w.
2. Divide w into l groups $G_1, \ldots, G_l$ of size k, where $l = \lfloor m/k \rfloor$.
3. For each group G_i, where $i = 1, \ldots, l$, do the following steps:
   (a) Set t_i as the number of '1' in the subgroup of G_i marked by h_i.
   (b) Set u_i as the size of subgroup h_i, i.e., number of '1' in h_i.
   (c) Set the group bit $b_i = 1$ if $t_i > u_i/2$ and set $b_i = 0$ if $t_i < u_i/2$. If $t_i = u_i/2$, set t_i randomly because of voting tie.
4. Output $b_1, \ldots, b_l$ as processed PUF response.

Note that in the DarkSMV method above, the size of the voting subgroup is not fixed. It depends on the number of dark bits in the group. Since the size of the subgroup may not be an odd number, we may need to break the voting tie using a random value, as in step 3(c) above.

We now evaluate the performance of our DarkSMV method using the dataset introduced in Section 3. For the dark-bit mask generation we choose 20 dark-bit reference measurements from the T=25°C, V=1.2V operating condition. Using the dark bit technique in isolation results in an mean intra-distance or error rate 0.75%, a reduction of more than 8x over the raw PUF error rate of 6.5%. The results of combining SMV with the dark bit technique are shown in Table 4 for DarkSMV parameters of $n = 512$ and $k = 9, 13, 17$.

Table 4. Experimental results for DarkSMV(20, k)

	μ_{intra}	σ_{intra}	max_{intra}	μ_{inter}	σ_{inter}	$\mu_{bias(ones)}$
$k=9$	.000202	.000652	.007812	.483790	.023894	.503783
$k=13$	.000028	.000242	.003906	.481679	.024121	.504234
$k=17$	.000012	.000179	.003906	.483748	.024117	.509123

The results show that DarkSMV results in significant further reductions in error rate over that obtained from dark bits in isolation. The mean intra-distance μ_{intra} shows reductions of over 90% while the max intra-distance max_{intra} is reduced to the sub-bit level even for $k = 9$. Figure 5 shows the inter- and intra-distance results for the $k = 13$ and $k = 17$ case.

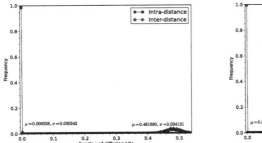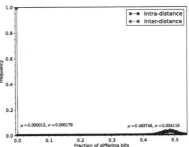

Fig. 5. Inter- vs intra-distances for DarkSMV, k=13 (left) and k=17 (right)

6 Applications of SMV

As we have shown in the last few sections, SMV can significantly reduce the PUF error rate. In this section, we discuss how low PUF error rates can benefit specific PUF applications. We use PUF-based key generation as a representative PUF application. According to [21,7,18], PUF-based key generation eliminates the need to store keys in the clear in non-volatile memory technologies such as fuses or flash. They are thus attractive in applications where high-assurance design techniques such tamper-resistant hardware are too expensive to deploy due to cost or form-factor considerations. Let $\mathcal{C}[n, k, d]$ be an error correcting code, where n is the length of the code, k is the size of message, and d is the minimum distance of the code. In order to extract a 128-bit key from the PUF, Bösch et al. suggested some fuzzy extractor constructions to extract 171-bit entropy from SRAM PUFs [3]. We list a few parameters from [3] in Table 5. We need approximately 4000 bits of PUF in order to extract 128 bits, assuming that PUF raw error rate is 15%. The failure probability represents the expected failure rate of the overall PUF-based key generation scheme.

Table 5. Parameters to extract a 128-bit cryptographic key for SRAM PUFs [3]

Error Correction Codes	PUF Size	Failure Probability
BCH[1020, 43, 439]	4080	1.44E-8
RM[32, 6, 16] & Rep[5, 1, 5]	4640	1.49E-6
Golay[24, 13, 7] & Rep[11, 1, 11]	3696	5.41E-7

Using the combined SMV and dark bits method described in Section 5, we can reduce the error rate significantly, thus reducing the need for expensive error correction codes. For example, using the result from Table 4, the error rate is reduced to 0.0002, 0.000028, and 0.000012, respectively, with $k = 9$, 13, and 17.

Table 6 shows the PUF and error correction parameters required to extract a 128-bit cryptographic key from an SRAM PUF. Note that, using the SMV group size $k = 9$, we only need a 2349-bit PUF and a simple BCH code BCH[29, 19, 5] to correct up to 2 bit errors per 29 bits. Using the SMV group size $k = 13$, we can use a simple Hamming code Hamming[7, 4, 3] as the error correction scheme, due to the low error rate. Implementing such Hamming code is almost free in hardware.

Table 6. Parameters to extract a 128-bit cryptographic key for SRAM PUFs using SMV and dark bits method

Method	Error Correction Codes	PUF Size	Failure Probability
DarkSMV(20, 9)	BCH[29, 19, 5]	2349	2.62E-7
DarkSMV(20, 13)	Hamming[7, 4, 3]	3913	7.08E-7
DarkSMV(20, 17)	Hamming[63, 57, 3]	3213	8.43E-7

Based on these results we believe that SMV is a valuable PUF pre-processing technique in situations where non-volatile storage is cheap (and may be off-chip) while the area cost for logic is expensive. In these scenarios it is beneficial to reduce the cost of ECC to a minimum.

7   Conclusion

In this paper we introduce a new PUF pre-processing technique we term Spatial Majority Voting (SMV). We show analytically SMV if effective in reducing the raw error rate of SRAM PUF responses to low levels and empirically confirm these results using test data obtained from a 65 nm SRAM PUF characterization vehicle. An alternative SMV scheme is introduced for biased PUF responses and shown to be effective for bias rates of up to 60%. Finally, we combine SMV with the dark bits method and show empirically that this approach is capable of reducing the PUF error rate to the sub-bit level where the required ECC complexity is significantly lowered, resulting in a reduced system cost for applications where minimizing logic-cost is the primary design constraint.

Acknowledgement. We thank Intrinsic-ID and EU FP7 programme UNIQUE for providing the SRAM PUF data which enabled the evaluation of our scheme. We thank the anonymous reviewers for providing helpful comments to this paper.

References

1. Armknecht, F., Maes, R., Sadeghi, A.-R., Sunar, B., Tuyls, P.: Memory leakage-resilient encryption based on physically unclonable functions. In: Matsui, M. (ed.) ASIACRYPT 2009. LNCS, vol. 5912, pp. 685–702. Springer, Heidelberg (2009)

2. Böhm, C., Hofer, M., Pribyl, W.: A microcontroller SRAM-PUF. In: 5th International Conference on Network and System Security, pp. 269–273. IEEE (2011)
3. Bösch, C., Guajardo, J., Sadeghi, A.-R., Shokrollahi, J., Tuyls, P.: Efficient helper data key extractor on FPGAs. In: Oswald, E., Rohatgi, P. (eds.) CHES 2008. LNCS, vol. 5154, pp. 181–197. Springer, Heidelberg (2008)
4. Brzuska, C., Fischlin, M., Schröder, H., Katzenbeisser, S.: Physically uncloneable functions in the universal composition framework. In: Rogaway, P. (ed.) CRYPTO 2011. LNCS, vol. 6841, pp. 51–70. Springer, Heidelberg (2011)
5. Dodis, Y., Reyzin, L., Smith, A.: Fuzzy extractors: How to generate strong keys from biometrics and other noisy data. In: Cachin, C., Camenisch, J.L. (eds.) EUROCRYPT 2004. LNCS, vol. 3027, pp. 523–540. Springer, Heidelberg (2004)
6. Gassend, B., Clarke, D., van Dijk, M., Devadas, S.: Silicon physical random functions. In: ACM Conference on Computer and Communications Security, pp. 148–160. ACM Press, New York (2002)
7. Guajardo, J., Kumar, S.S., Schrijen, G.-J., Tuyls, P.: FPGA Intrinsic PUFs and Their Use for IP Protection. In: Paillier, P., Verbauwhede, I. (eds.) CHES 2007. LNCS, vol. 4727, pp. 63–80. Springer, Heidelberg (2007)
8. Juels, A., Wattenberg, M.: A fuzzy commitment scheme. In: ACM Conference on Computer and Communications Security (CCS), pp. 28–36. ACM (1999)
9. Katzenbeisser, S., Kocabaş, Ü., Rožić, V., Sadeghi, A.-R., Verbauwhede, I., Wachsmann, C.: PUFs: Myth, fact or busted? A security evaluation of physically unclonable functions (PUFs) cast in silicon. In: Prouff, E., Schaumont, P. (eds.) CHES 2012. LNCS, vol. 7428, pp. 283–301. Springer, Heidelberg (2012)
10. Koeberl, P., Li, J., Rajan, A., Vishik, C., Wu, W.: A practical device authentication scheme using SRAM PUFS. In: McCune, J.M., Balacheff, B., Perrig, A., Sadeghi, A.-R., Sasse, A., Beres, Y. (eds.) TRUST 2011. LNCS, vol. 6740, pp. 63–77. Springer, Heidelberg (2011)
11. Kumar, S.S., Guajardo, J., Maes, R., Schrijen, G.J., Tuyls, P.: The butterfly PUF: Protecting IP on every FPGA. In: IEEE International Workshop on Hardware-Oriented Security and Trust (HOST), pp. 67–70 (June 2008)
12. Lee, J.W., Lim, D., Gassend, B., Edward Suh, G., van Dijk, M., Devadas, S.: A technique to build a secret key in integrated circuits for identification and authentication application. In: Proceedings of the Symposium on VLSI Circuits, pp. 176–179 (2004)
13. van der Leest, V., Preneel, B., van der Sluis, E.: Soft decision error correction for compact memory-based PUFS using a single enrollment. In: Prouff, E., Schaumont, P. (eds.) CHES 2012. LNCS, vol. 7428, pp. 268–282. Springer, Heidelberg (2012)
14. Lim, D., Lee, J.W., Gassend, B., Edward Suh, G., van Dijk, M., Devadas, S.: Extracting secret keys from integrated circuits. IEEE Transactions on Very Large Scale Integration (VLSI) Systems 13(10), 1200–1205 (2005)
15. Maes, R., Rozic, V., Verbauwhede, I., Koeberl, P., van der Sluis, E., van der Leest, V.: Experimental evaluation of physically unclonable functions in 65 nm cmos. In: 2012 Proceedings of the ESSCIRC (ESSCIRC), pp. 486–489 (September 2012)
16. Maes, R., Van Herrewege, A., Verbauwhede, I.: PUFKY: A fully functional PUF-based cryptographic key generator. In: Prouff, E., Schaumont, P. (eds.) CHES 2012. LNCS, vol. 7428, pp. 302–319. Springer, Heidelberg (2012)
17. Maes, R., Tuyls, P., Verbauwhede, I.: Intrinsic PUFs from flip-flops on reconfigurable devices. In: 3rd Benelux Workshop on Information and System Security (WISSec 2008), Eindhoven, NL, p. 17 (2008)

18. Maes, R., Tuyls, P., Verbauwhede, I.: Low-overhead implementation of a soft decision helper data algorithm for SRAM PUFs. In: Clavier, C., Gaj, K. (eds.) CHES 2009. LNCS, vol. 5747, pp. 332–347. Springer, Heidelberg (2009)
19. Pappu, R.S.: Physical one-way functions. PhD thesis, Massachusetts Institute of Technology (March 2001)
20. Simons, P., van der Sluis, E., van der Leest, V.: Buskeeper PUFs, a promising alternative to D Flip-Flop PUFs. In: 2012 IEEE International Symposium on Hardware-Oriented Security and Trust (HOST), pp. 7–12 (June 2012)
21. Simpson, E., Schaumont, P.: Offline hardware/Software authentication for reconfigurable platforms. In: Goubin, L., Matsui, M. (eds.) CHES 2006. LNCS, vol. 4249, pp. 311–323. Springer, Heidelberg (2006)
22. Edward Suh, G., Devadas, S.: Physical unclonable functions for device authentication and secret key generation. In: Design Automation Conference, pp. 9–14. ACM Press, New York (2007)
23. Yu, M.-D., Devadas, S.: Secure and robust error correction for physical unclonable functions. IEEE Design Test of Computers 27(1), 48–65 (2010)

A   Analysis of Naïve SMV

In this section, we analyze the efficiency of the naïve SMV scheme. In naïve SMV, majority voting is performed on all bits in a group: if there are more '1', then '1' is output as the group bit, otherwise '0'. Since the PUF results are random and exhibit little bias, a single flip in the bits with the majority value will overturn the result of majority voting.

Let p be the PUF bit error rate. Let ℓ_0 be the total number of zeros in the group. Let x be the total number of bit flips in the group, among them x_0 is the number of $0 \to 1$ flips and x_1 is for $1 \to 0$ flips, where $x_0 + x_1 = x$. The number of zeros in an evaluated result of the group equals to $\ell_0' = \ell_0 - x_0 + x_1$. A majority voting fault is defined as the condition of '0' as majority bit differing before and after the evaluation.

$$\mathrm{Flip}(\ell, \ell_0, x_0, x_1) = ((\ell_0 > \lfloor \ell/2 \rfloor) \oplus (\ell_0 - x_0 + x_1) > \lfloor \ell/2 \rfloor) = \mathbf{true})$$

The probability of a group bit error which is the probability of a majority voting flip is defined as:

$$P_{\mathrm{group}} = \sum_{0 \le \ell_0 \le \ell} \sum_{0 \le x \le \ell} \sum_{0 \le x_0 \le x} \mathrm{Flip}(\ell, \ell_0, x_0, x - x_0) \cdot \mathbf{p_1} \cdot \mathbf{p_2} \cdot \mathbf{p_3}$$

Where the three conditional probabilities are defined as following, and P_0 and P_1 are the probability that a bit is equal to 0 and 1 respectively:

1. $\mathbf{p_1}$: the probability of having ℓ_0 0's out of ℓ-bit voting group: $\binom{\ell}{\ell_0} P_0^{\ell_0} P_1^{\ell - \ell_0}$
2. $\mathbf{p_2}$: the probability of having x bit flips in a ℓ-bit group: $\binom{\ell}{x} p^x (1-p)^{\ell-x}$
3. $\mathbf{p_3}$: the probability of having x_0 flips to be $0 \to 1$ flip: $\binom{\ell_0}{x_0}\binom{\ell-\ell_0}{x-x_0}/\binom{\ell}{x}$

Figure 1 (right) shows the P_{group} under different group sizes and PUF error rate p ranging from 1% to 20%. The PUF evaluation results are evenly distributed, i.e. $P_0 = P_1 = 0.5$. The larger PUF bit error rate leads to a larger group error rate. The blue dashed line illustrates the error rate with group size 1 or no grouping. It's obvious that grouping is bad in terms of error rate, as the grouping size increases the rate increases as well. Due to the small bias of the PUF bit value, the number of '0' and '1' are so close that voting is performed at the borderline, any small disturbance may easily change the voting result.

Active File Integrity Monitoring
Using Paravirtualized Filesystems

Michael Velten[1], Sascha Wessel[1], Frederic Stumpf[1], and Claudia Eckert[2]

[1] Fraunhofer Research Institution for Applied and Integrated Security
Munich, Germany
{michael.velten,sascha.wessel,frederic.stumpf}@aisec.fraunhofer.de
[2] Technische Universität München, Computer Science Department
Munich, Germany
claudia.eckert@in.tum.de

Abstract. Monitoring file integrity and preventing illegal modifications is a crucial part of improving system security. Unfortunately, current research focusing on isolating monitoring components from supervised systems can often still be thwarted by tampering with the hooks placed inside of Virtual Machines (VMs), thus resulting in critical file operations not being noticed. In this paper, we present an approach of relocating a supervised VM's entire filesystem into the isolated realm of the host. This way, we can enforce that all file operations originating from a VM (e.g., read and write operations) must necessarily be routed through the hypervisor, and thus can be tracked and even be prevented. Disabling hooks in the VM then becomes pointless as this would render a VM incapable of accessing or manipulating its own filesystem. This guarantees secure and complete active file integrity monitoring of VMs. The experimental results of our prototype implementation show the feasibility of our approach.

Keywords: File Integrity Protection, Active File Integrity Monitoring, Paravirtualized Filesystem.

1 Introduction

Protecting the integrity of file objects is a fundamental security objective for building trustworthy systems and for counteracting malware threats. A prominent example of achieving file integrity protection is the Host-based Intrusion Detection System (HIDS) Tripwire [1], which detects manipulations to filesystem objects by comparing their hash values to reference hash values in periodic intervals. However, the problem with Tripwire and similar approaches, including Linux Security Modules (LSM) based approaches like SELinux [2], is that critical security components (e.g., the monitoring components) are not encapsulated from the supervised system. This allows malware to attack and disable the monitoring components in order to conceal attack traces or to hide their presence altogether.

R. Bloem and P. Lipp (Eds.): INTRUST 2013, LNCS 8292, pp. 53–69, 2013.

Researchers have proposed architectures utilizing virtualization to encapsulate the critical security components from the supervised system. The supervised system is moved into a separate VM while the monitoring components are isolated and placed outside of the VM [3, 4]. This prevents malware located in the VM from attacking and disabling the external monitoring components. In order to bridge the semantic gap introduced by the virtualization layer, Virtual Machine Introspection (VMI) techniques are being deployed for monitoring the VMs. Security tools such as [5, 6] build upon VMI and similar techniques for supervising guest VMs. However, these tools realize only *passive* monitoring. This means that security-relevant events occurring within a VM will be recognized after they have happened. In particular, passive monitoring is unable to intercept on events and prevent them from happening. To overcome this problem, researchers have proposed *active* monitoring where hooks are placed inside the monitored VMs. These hooks allow to interrupt the control flow within a VM and give control to the hypervisor before a critical event actually happens [7–9]. However, malware can often circumvent active monitoring by tampering with the hooks placed inside the VMs, thus resulting in critical file operations not being noticed on the hypervisor-level.

In this paper, we present our approach of relocating a supervised VM's entire filesystem into the isolated realm of the host. The only way of accessing and manipulating a VM's filesystem is by communicating with a privileged component located in the hypervisor which has exclusive access to the VM's filesystem. Therefore, the hypervisor is guaranteed that all file operations originating from a VM (e.g., read and write operations) are necessarily routed through the hypervisor. This allows us to actively monitor all file I/O operations within a VM in real-time from "outside of the box" and to possibly prevent them from happening. Furthermore, this approach solves the aforementioned problem of having malware disable hooks in the VM as this would render the VM (and as such the malware itself) incapable of accessing or manipulating the VM's filesystem. The communication between guest VMs and the hypervisor is done over the paravirtualized Plan 9 filesystem protocol [10], which has the advantage of efficiently bridging the semantic gap and preserving all relevant file operation information. Finally, we build upon and improve the work done in [11] to securely measure all executed binaries of all VMs and store these measurements in a single, multiplexed Trusted Platform Module (TPM). This allows for attesting the integrity of individual VMs in the course of a remote attestation. Another key feature of our approach is that we enable regular users of VMs to autonomously install and upgrade software packages in a secure and controlled manner without the need of requiring the intervention of the administrator of the physical system.

The rest of this paper is organized as follows. Section 2 states our assumptions and attacker model. Section 3 explains in detail our concept for active monitoring of guest VMs. Section 4 describes our prototype implementation. Section 5 presents our performance evaluation results. Section 6 gives the security analysis. Section 7 discusses related work. Section 8 concludes this paper.

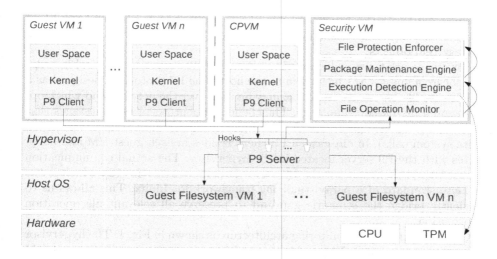

Fig. 1. Paravirtualized monitoring architecture with externalized guest filesystems

2 Assumptions and Attacker Model

We assume a virtualized platform where attackers have full access to their respective guest VMs, but no direct physical hardware access. We consider remote attackers as well as legitimate users of guest VMs that try to compromise the guest VM and gain control of the guest user space and kernel. We focus on preventing malicious file manipulations, which includes temporary as well as persistent file modifications that survive reboots (e.g., the installation of malware). Another objective is to prevent the execution of unknown and malicious executables, respectively. We do not consider runtime attacks, e.g., in-memory modifications, buffer overflow attacks, and code injection.

3 Active Monitoring of Guest VMs

The key aspect of our concept is that we relocate a guest VM's entire filesystem from the guest VM to the isolated realm of the host. We then grant only a privileged component, located in the hypervisor, exclusive access to the guest filesystems. This means that for all guest VMs, the only way of accessing and manipulating their own filesystems is by communicating with this privileged component located in the hypervisor. Therefore, the hypervisor is guaranteed that all file operations originating from a VM (e.g., read and write operations) are necessarily routed through the hypervisor. This allows the hypervisor to actively monitor all file operations of all guest VMs and to possibly prevent them before they actually happen. Furthermore, this makes sure that it is impossible for an attacker to bypass the hypervisor (and as such circumvent the monitoring), even in the event of a completely compromised VM – since otherwise there is no way of accessing the VM's filesystem. This is an advantage over other approaches (e.g., [7] and [8]) where disabling hooks in the VM still allows for manipulation of filesystem objects.

For our concept, we make use of the Plan 9 (P9) filesystem protocol in order to relocate a guest VM's filesystem to the host. The P9 protocol is designed as a distributed filesystem protocol that may be used over the network and which operates on a file-based granularity. The client-server protocol uses messages that reflect ordinary file operations (for example, messages originating from read or write system calls). In our case, a P9 client resides in each guest VM and cooperates with the P9 server located in the hypervisor. The actual communication between the P9 clients and the P9 server is done over virtio [12], which is the de-facto standard of a paravirtualizing framework for Linux. This allows us to efficiently bridge the semantic gap and to preserve all relevant file operation information.

Our paravirtualized monitoring architecture is shown in Fig. 1. The hypervisor runs one or more guest VMs, which are subject to monitoring. Each guest VM contains a P9 client that translates ordinary file operation requests originating from within the VM to P9 request messages. These messages will be forwarded by the respective P9 client to the P9 server located in the realm of the hypervisor. The P9 server has exclusive access to the filesystems of the guest VMs. The guest filesystems are located on the filesystem of the host. The P9 server processes the P9 requests accordingly, for example, by reading a file (and providing it to the P9 client) or by writing to the filesystem. Note that we prohibit the loading of kernel modules within VMs in order to prevent attacks utilizing filesystem caching (cf. Section 6). In particular, we prevent the loading of kernel modules supporting other filesystems, including virtual and stacked filesystems, as well as modules enabling filesystems in userspace (e.g., FUSE).

There are four components responsible for monitoring and enforcing file integrity of the guests. The monitoring components are encapsulated from the guest VMs (and the hypervisor) in a special security VM (cf. Fig. 1). We place hooks in all relevant parts of the request handlers of the P9 server in order to inform the monitoring components of all relevant file operations. This enables the security VM to monitor all requests originating from a VM's P9 client trying to access its guest filesystem. The components process the P9 requests and decide – based on an access control policy – whether a request will be granted or denied. In particular, the monitoring components are:

File Operation Monitor (FOM). Receives and analyzes all hooked P9 request messages from the P9 server. Relevant requests will be forwarded to EDE and PME (see below). The details are described in Section 3.1.

Execution Detection Engine (EDE). Detects when a guest VM is trying to execute a file based on a heuristic approach which is based on recognizing distinct sequences of P9 requests. Execution of files will be securely recorded by storing a corresponding *SHA*1 hash value in a secure element, in particular, a TPM [13]. The details are described in Section 3.3.

Table 1. Critical Requests of the Plan 9 9P2000.L protocol

P9 Request	Potential Impact
write	Writing new files or modifying the content of existing files, e.g., altering configuration files or executables
rename, renameat	Moving files, thus effectively deleting them from one location within the filesystem and possibly replacing other files with the content of the renamed file
remove, unlinkat	Removing files or directories, e.g., changing the behavior of programs by deleting their configuration files or hiding traces by deleting log files
lcreate, mkdir	Creating new files or directories; may be misused to truncate existing files
link, symlink	Creating a hardlink or symbolic link, e.g., creating a link in a directory like /bin to a malicious executable in /tmp (where the creation of arbitrary files may be allowed)

Package Maintenance Engine (PME). Detects when a guest VM is trying to install, remove, upgrade, or downgrade software packages, and handles it by utilizing a special VM, called the Complementary Privileged Virtual Machine (CPVM). The details are described in Section 3.4.

File Protection Enforcer (FPE). Decides whether a P9 request will finally be granted or denied. The decision is based on whitelist policy rules. The details are described in Section 3.2.

3.1   Monitoring and Analyzing File Operation Requests

The File Operation Monitor (FOM) is responsible for analyzing P9 request messages forwarded by the P9 server. In particular, FOM scans for all *critical requests* of the utilized 9P2000.L[1] protocol [14]. A request is considered critical if it has the potential to impact the integrity of the guest's filesystem. Table 1 lists all critical P9 requests that are handled by FOM along with a description of their potential impacts.

Note that Table 1 does not list the P9 **read** request since it cannot be used to affect a file's integrity. However, **read** requests still play an important part in our concept as they occur as a distinct sequence of P9 requests whenever a file in the guest VM is going to be executed. Since the P9 filesystem protocol does not incorporate a dedicated **execute** request itself, we take advantage of this sequence of **read** signature requests in order to come up with a heuristic to detect the execution of files. The details are described in Section 3.3.

Shadow Copy Write. The P9 **write** request requires further consideration. A special case of the **write** request is that it may exceed the message size of

---

[1] 9P2000.L includes the core 9P2000 requests as a subset.

the P9 client or the P9 server implementation (or both). The reason is that the entire (to be written) payload data has to be sent from the P9 client to the P9 server. In such cases, the P9 client splits up a `write` request $w[f, d]$ (containing the payload data d for a file f) into several sub-requests $w_1[f, d_1], \ldots, w_n[f, d_n]$ [14]. This poses a problem for monitoring `write` requests because FPE may not be able to decide upon the partial information of a sub-request $w_i[f, d_i]$ (in particular, the first sub-request $w_1[f, d_1]$) on whether the overall request $w[f, d]$ should be granted or not. In particular, if FPE only allows a file f to be written if its future content (i.e., the content of f after applying the `write` operation $w[f, d]$) matches a certain hash value (cf. Section 3.2), knowledge of the entire future content of f is required in order to be able to calculate the hash value of f. Note that in this regard, it is not sufficient to only consider the payload data d. The reason is that a `write` request may only partially write a file f. In this case, the payload data d differs from the content of the resulting file f.

We solve this problem by introducing a technique called *shadowing*, which works in three phases:

1. FOM detects a `write` sub-request $w_1[f, d_1]$ by inspecting the request's header data. If f already exists on the guest's filesystem, FOM creates a *shadow copy* f' with the same content as f. If f does not exist, FOM creates an empty file f'. The shadow copy f' is located outside of the guest's filesystem and only accessible by FOM. Depending on the size of f, and possibly other factors (e.g., hardware and performance constraints), the shadow copy may be kept entirely in RAM.

2. FOM applies the sub-request $w_1[f, d_1]$ along with all other corresponding sub-requests $w_2[f, d_2], \ldots, w_n[f, d_n]$ exclusively to the shadow copy f'. When all sub-requests $w_1[f, d_1], \ldots, w_n[f, d_n]$ have been processed (which is detected by a terminal `clunk` or `fsync` operation [10]), FOM signals to FPE that there is a new `write` request $w[f, d]$ and passes a pointer to f'.

3. FPE is then able to calculate the hash value of f', which resembles the potential future content of f, and to finally decide whether the overall `write` request $w[f, d]$ should be granted or denied. If it is granted, the P9 server eventually gets signaled to allow and process all sub-requests $w_1[f, d_1], \ldots, w_n[f, d_n]$. Finally, the shadow copy f' gets discarded.

3.2   Enforcing File Protection

The File Protection Enforcer (FPE) is responsible for deciding whether a P9 request will be granted or denied. The decision making is based on Access Control List (ACLs) that define which filesystem operations are allowed within guests and which ones are prohibited. An ACL consists of arbitrarily many Access Control Entries (ACEs) which determine for a given file f whether certain operations on f are allowed or denied. There exists one ACL for each VM. The ACL implements a whitelist approach that prohibits all filesystem operations within a VM unless an operation is explicitly granted by an ACE.

Table 2. Critical requests mapped to policy checks using only predicates

P9 Request	Predicate Policy Check
write(f,d)	$f' \leftarrow w[f,d] : W(f) \wedge H(f')$
rename(f_1,f_2), renameat(f_1,f_2)	$W(f_2) \wedge D(f_1) \wedge H(f_1)$
remove(f), unlinkat(f)	$D(f)$
lcreate(f)	$W(f)$
link(f_1,f_2), symlink(f_1,f_2)	$W(f_2) \wedge H(f_1)$
exec(f) (*)	$E(f) \wedge H(f)$

(*) virtual request

Policy Predicates and P9 Request Mapping. We define a minimal set of four predicates that may be used to construct an ACE. All predicates evaluate to either true or false. The predicates are:

$W(f)$: (partial) writing of file f allowed?
$D(f)$: deletion of file f allowed?
$E(f)$: execution of file f allowed?
$H(f)$: hash sum of the content of file f matches a reference hash value?

The objective of exclusively using this minimal set of predicates in the ACEs, is to abstract from the actual P9 requests and to come up with simpler, more generic ACEs. This has the advantage that one does not have to create ACEs for each specific P9 request. Instead, it is only required to define for a file f whether writing $W(f)$, deletion $D(f)$, and execution $E(f)$ is allowed or denied (the latter of which is the default) – possibly in conjunction with reference hash values that have to be matched ($H(f)$). In particular, a file may be associated with a list of one or more *reference hash values* $\langle h_1, \ldots, h_n \rangle$. The predicate $H(f)$ evaluates to true iff the content of f matches one of the hash values h_i or if the list of reference hash values contains the wildcard character "*". Otherwise, $H(f)$ always evaluates to false.

For example, an ACE for a file f may define that writing of f is allowed (W predicate) if the resulting content matches one of several reference hash values (H predicate). Such an ACE may then evaluate to true not only for P9 write requests but also for rename, renameat, lcreate, link, and symlink requests, respectively, as will be explained in the following.

For the actual policy enforcement, the FPE internally maps all critical P9 requests (cf. Table 1) to corresponding policy checks using only these predicates. The mapping is shown in Table 2 (for clarity, we only illustrate the policy checks for files and omit the checks for directories). If the overall expression of such a policy check evaluates to true, the respective P9 request will be granted by FPE. Otherwise, it will be denied. Note that a write request $w[f, d]$ (which might be a partial write) will first be applied to a temporary file f' (denoted by $f' \leftarrow w[f, d]$ in Table 2). This is similar to shadowing as described in Section 3.1. If the content of the resulting file f' matches a valid reference hash value, $H(f')$ evaluates to *true*. Also note that exec is not an actual P9 request but a *virtual request* which is propagated by EDE. This is explained in Section 3.3.

Package Policy Rules. We also define predicates to determine which software package maintenance operations may be autonomously issued by legitimate guest VM users (cf. Section 3.4). The predicates are:

$P_i(p)$: installing, upgrading, or downgrading package p allowed?
$P_r(p)$: removing package p allowed?
$P_h(p)$: hash sum of the package p matches a reference hash value?

Whenever PME detects an installation, upgrading, or downgrading attempt of a package p (cf. Section 3.4), respectively, it is propagated to FPE which, in turn, will check whether the predicate $P_i(p)$ evaluates to true. Furthermore, the predicate $P_h(p)$ may be used – analogously to $H(f)$ as described above – to restrict the installation, upgrading, and downgrading of a package p to packages that match a reference hash value. This allows to selectively permit only certain packages (and package versions) while prohibiting others, e.g., older versions with known vulnerabilities. For removing attempts of p, FPE will check whether the predicate $P_r(p)$ evaluates to true.

3.3   Detecting Program Execution

Detecting and possibly preventing the execution of files within VMs is an important part of our concept. Unfortunately, having EDE detect executed programs from outside of the guest VMs is not straight forward due to the fact that P9 does not distinguish between reading a file and executing a file. Instead, in both cases a read request is sent by the P9 client and only the VM decides afterwards whether the read file will be executed. Note that we cannot just extend the P9 clients (and server) such that they distinguish between read and execute requests (e.g., an executable-bit). The reason is that this information would not be trustworthy since an attacker may tamper with it (e.g., setting the executable-bit from 1 to 0) once the VM is compromised. Therefore, we incorporate EDE which is able to detect the execution of a file within a VM by utilizing a heuristic approach. EDE is protected from the aforementioned attacks since it is located in the security VM (cf. Fig. 1) and monitors the VMs from "outside of the box", without relying on auxiliary (untrustworthy) information sent from the VM.

Whenever a program is going to be executed within a VM, there will be a distinct sequence of preceding Plan 9 requests in a defined chronological order, as described in the following. EDE recognizes this sequence of *signature requests* and deduces which file is intended to be executed. FPE may then grant or deny the execution based on policy rules as described in Section 3.2.

For the execution detection, we consider the Executable and Linking Format (ELF) [15], which is the standard binary format for executables on many Unix-like operating systems, including Linux. The heuristic for detecting the execution of ELF files under Linux, consists of the following signature requests (in their chronological order of occurrence):

1. The **execve** system call first reads in 128 bytes to determine the binary type of a file f. Consequently, EDE scans for the corresponding P9 read requests.
2. The ELF loader of the Linux kernel invokes the function **kernel_read**, which reads 224 bytes from f, starting from offset 52.
3. A subsequent invocation of **kernel_read** reads 19 bytes from f, starting from offset 276, which gets treated as the path to an interpreter [15].

The above signature requests are usually followed by multiple read requests that attempt to map the entire file f into memory. Note that EDE is also able to detect the loading of ELF libraries, which generate signature requests similar to that of executed binaries. We consider the detection of executed script files (e.g., shell scripts) out of the scope of this paper. This will be addressed in future research.

Secure Storage of Integrity Measurements. We build upon and improve the work done in [11] to measure all executed binaries of all VMs and store these measurements in a single, multiplexed TPM. This allows for attesting the integrity of individual VMs (*remote attestation*). In [11], each VM runs an adapted version of the Integrity Measurement Architecture (IMA) [16] that monitors the execution of files, calculates integrity measurements, and forwards them to a TPM multiplexing agent located in the hypervisor. We improve this solution by relocating and consolidating the IMA measurement components from the guest VMs to the well encapsulated security VM. This has the advantage that only a single measurement agent is required for monitoring the execution of files of all VMs from "outside of the box" and for storing integrity measurements (*SHA*1 values) in the TPM. Additionally, this prevents attackers from tampering with the monitoring and measuring components, respectively, since they are out of reach of the guest VMs. In our case, measuring all monitored executables and storing them in the TPM is done by EDE.

3.4 Autonomous Software Package Installation and Upgrade

Another key feature of our approach is that it is possible for legitimate users of guest VMs to autonomously install, remove, upgrade, or downgrade software packages without the need of any manual intervention by the administrator of the physical system. However, these *package maintenance operations* are not allowed to be done in an arbitrary manner, but all such operations have to adhere to the policy rules enforced by FPE as described in Section 3.2. Also note that it is not possible for a guest VM user to directly manipulate the package contents as they are write protected. This prevents illegal modifications of the guest VM by attackers – which includes legitimate but maliciously acting VM users. Finally, note that PME may also actively enforce the upgrading of (outdated) packages within VMs.

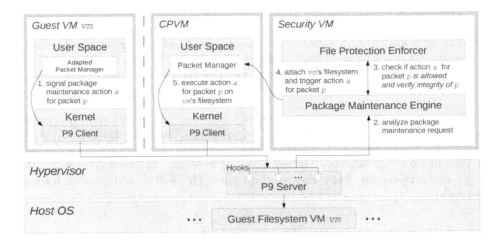

Fig. 2. Installation and upgrading of packages via CPVM

The work flow for installing, removing, upgrading, and downgrading software packages is depicted in Fig. 2 and will be described in the following.

i) Signaling of Package Maintenance Request. First, a legitimate user of the guest VM executes the package manager within the VM with the corresponding maintenance action a (and parameters) for a package p (step 1 of Fig. 2). The request is forwarded by the P9 client to the P9 server. The Package Maintenance Engine (PME) located in the security VM catches and analyzes the package maintenance request (step 2). In this regard, it is important to note that PME considers all information gathered from the guest VM as untrustworthy. This means that even if an attacker compromised the guest VM, it is not possible for him to use the package manager to send fake information in a way that would allow the circumvention of the policy rules or the malfunctioning of any other security-critical component outside of the guest VM.

ii) Checking Package Integrity and Permissions. PME sends a query to FPE in order to determine whether p is a known and valid package on which the requested action a may be applied. Hence, FPE first checks if the action a on package p is allowed for the respective VM by evaluating the P_i and P_r predicates of the corresponding ACE. Following this, FPE verifies the integrity of the package p by evaluating the $P_h(p)$ predicate of the corresponding ACE (cf. Section 3.2). The usage of reference hash values allows to selectively permit only certain packages – and package versions – while prohibiting others (e.g., older versions with known vulnerabilities) that may otherwise be exploited by an attacker to compromise the system. If the hash value is not valid, the maintenance process is aborted and an error is signaled to the package manager of the guest VM.

iii) Executing Package Maintenance Request. The package maintenance process for all guest VMs is executed in a special VM, called the Complementary Privileged Virtual Machine (CPVM). The CPVM runs in parallel to the guest VMs and has exclusive permission to install, remove, upgrade, or downgrade packages of all VMs. A key feature of the CPVM is that it operates (via the P9 protocol) on the same filesystem (located in the host) as the guest VM vm that triggered the respective package maintenance request. This is achieved by attaching vm's filesystem (on the fly) to CPVM, for the duration of the package management process. This way, all package management operations done by CPVM are immediately visible to vm, and vice versa. This prevents synchronization problems and guarantees that both VMs always operate on the same state of the VM (e.g., information on which packages are installed, package versions, configuration file settings, etc.). Note that the guest VMs only require minimal (non-security critical) user space modifications of the package management tools (cf. Section 4.1) but no kernel modifications.

In the following, we justify the execution of the package maintenance operations within CPVM as opposed to executing them in the guest VM itself. The latter case could be achieved by having FPE properly adjust the policy rules such that the creation, deletion, modification etc. of files belonging to a certain package would be temporarily permitted for a certain VM. However, many modern package managing tools also allow packages (e.g., Debian packages, as used in our prototype implementation in Section 4.1) to contain script files that will be executed before and after a package maintenance operation, respectively. Parsing these script files (which may contain arbitrarily complex commands) and extracting their complete semantics (in order to be able to have FPE temporarily grant the corresponding file operations) is a highly complex task. Possible workarounds include disallowing such scripts or imposing certain constraints on their contents. However, this would prevent taking advantage of real-life packages as shipped with modern Unix-like operating systems. Our CPVM approach solves the aforementioned problems, yet it is fully compatible with full-fledged Unix-like operating systems (e.g., Linux distributions such as Debian).

Note that our approach does not require to suspend or pause a guest VM vm while CPVM is executing its software management operations on vm's filesystem but both VMs can run in parallel. This is due to the fact that both VMs communicate with the same P9 server – which deals with the correct synchronization of P9 requests. As such, the functioning of vm and CPVM is comparable to two (especially encapsulated) processes operating on the same filesystem within the realm of an ordinary operating system.

4   Implementation

We have implemented a prototype using the Native Linux KVM Tool (KVM) [17], version 3.1.rc7, with enabled KVM full virtualization support. In contrast to QEMU-KVM [18, 19], KVM has the goal to provide a clean, from-scratch, lightweight KVM host tool with only the minimal amount of legacy device emulation [17]. KVM ships with a P9 file server utilizing the virtio framework [12] for communicating with the P9 clients residing in the guest VMs. The P9 client functionality is provided by the v9fs client of the Linux kernel, which supports both the standard 9P2000 protocol and the extended 9P2000.L protocol, the latter of which we use.

Our host system runs Ubuntu 12.10. Each guest VM runs Debian 6.0 with Linux kernel 3.5.0 and enabled virtio and P9 support. The Linux guest kernel images reside on the host filesystem and will be passed as a parameter to KVM whenever a new VM is started. The security VM and CPVM also run Debian 6.0 with Linux kernel 3.5.0. The attached guest filesystem of CPVM is passed to KVM as a reference to a symbolic link. PME redirects this symbolic link dynamically to other guest filesystems as required by package maintenance requests.

The P9 server hooking functionality is realized by patching all relevant request handlers of the P9 virtio implementation so that FOM gets signaled and forwarded all required information. FOM and EDE are implemented in C. PME and FPE are implemented using a combination of Python scripts and shell scripts. Furthermore, FPE utilizes SQLite3 for efficiently managing our policy rules.

4.1   Installation and Upgrading of Packages via CPVM

As already mentioned, the guest VMs run Debian, which ships with the package management tools *dpkg* and *apt-get*. Since we do not allow guests to directly install, remove, upgrade, or downgrade packages on their own (cf. Section 3.4), we replace the user space tools *dpkg* and *apt-get* with our own versions $dpkg^R$ and apt-get^R, respectively, both of which forward all package maintenance requests to PME via the P9 protocol. To avoid having to modify or extend the P9 protocol, we just take advantage of regular P9 requests (that will be treated specially by PME) in order to pass the information of package management action, parameters, and package name. In particular, we utilize the P9 mkdir request (cf. Table 1) because it allows us to transfer all required information. PME parses the request and queries FPE on whether the action for package p is allowed and whether p is a valid package. If the request gets granted by FPE, PME places a file (called a *job*) in a special directory which is only accessible by CPVM. The job contains the respective command that will be executed by the privileged CPVM as soon as CPVM gets scheduled by PME. PME attaches the filesystem of the respective guest VM to CPVM and schedules CPVM. Eventually, CPVM detects the new job and executes it. Upon successful completion of the job, PME grants the P9 mkdir request to signal to $dpkg^R$ and apt-get^R, respectively, that the package maintenance request has been successfully executed.

5   Performance Evaluation

We assess the performance of our prototype implementation by measuring its write and read performance, and by comparing the results to three other

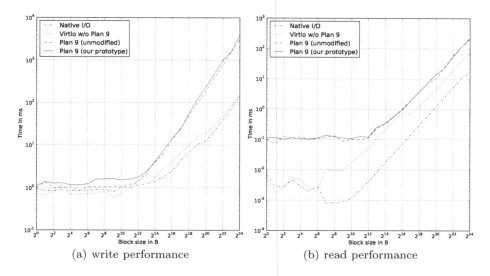

(a) write performance   (b) read performance

Fig. 3. Comparison of write and read performance of different environments

environments. The testing hardware consists of a PC with an Intel Core i7-2640M 2.8GHz CPU, 4 GB RAM, and an Intel SSDSA2BW160G3L solid-state drive containing an ext4 filesystem with a block size of 4kB.

Fig. 3 shows our testing results of the (a) write performance and (b) read performance benchmarks. We conducted the write and read operations with block sizes from 1B of up to 16MB (2^{24}B) and disabled caching.

The write performance is depicted in Fig. 3a. The time (in ms) to write data is given as a function of the block size (in bytes). All four examined environments – native I/O, virtio block without P9, unmodified P9 (plain P9), and our prototype – perform similarly up to block sizes of approx. 8kB (2^{13}B). For larger block sizes, the P9 environments perform worse than native I/O and virtio block. However, in our usage scenario such larger block sizes are negligible since I/O operations are usually done in block sizes of typical filesystems – which normally lie in the range of 512B to 4kB (which is also the maximum block size for ext4 on most architectures). There is no significant performance difference between plain P9 and our prototype.

As for the read performance (Fig. 3b), the results look as expected: native I/O takes the least time to read blocks, followed by virtio block, followed by the P9 environments – which inherently have the biggest performance overhead. However, analogous to the write performance, there is no significant performance difference between plain P9 and our prototype.

6   Security Analysis

In the following, we discuss attacks that target the persistent and non-persistent manipulation of files as well as the circumvention of the execution detection.

An attacker may try to persistently manipulate files within a VM and prevent the propagation of the changes to the P9 server, thus undermining active monitoring. A possible approach would be to compromise the guest kernel and tamper with the P9 client such that certain (or all) P9 messages will be blocked from being propagated to the P9 server. However, as explained in Section 3, all file operation requests must necessarily be routed through the P9 server because otherwise it is impossible for a guest VM to access the VM's filesystem.

For non-persistent file manipulations, an attacker may cache the filesystem (or parts thereof) locally in RAM and only work on this cached data (e.g., writing files in memory), thus undermining active monitoring. We protect against these kind of attacks by prohibiting the loading of kernel modules. In particular, we prevent the loading of kernel modules supporting other filesystems, including virtual and stacked filesystems, as well as modules enabling filesystems in userspace (e.g., FUSE). Attacking the kernel itself is only possible with runtime attacks (e.g., code injection), which is excluded by our attacker model (cf. Section 2).

For circumventing execution detection by EDE (cf. Section 3.3), an attacker might also employ stacked filesystems. However, we prevent attacks involving stacked filesystems by prohibiting the loading of kernel modules as described above. An attacker may also try to circumvent the execution detection by first mapping an entire file into memory and then executing it from RAM. There exist orthogonal techniques for preventing such attacks (e.g., [20, 21]), which we consider out of the scope of this paper. As mentioned in Section 3.3, we currently do not consider the detection of executed script files (e.g., shell scripts). However, this is not due to a limitation of our architecture but is rather a matter of effort to extend the heuristic in future research.

7   Related Work

Tripwire [1] is a commonly known HIDS, which detects changes to filesystem objects by checking the filesystem in periodic intervals. However, there is no support for real-time checking. Hence, Tripwire cannot *prevent* attacks but just detect them after they have happened. Furthermore, Tripwire is not encapsulated from the monitored system and as such is susceptible to attacks. I^{3}FS [22] tries to improve Tripwire by adding real-time integrity checks. However, since the supervising agent and the relevant databases are located within the realm of the monitored system, I^{3}FS is also vulnerable to attacks.

In [9], Zhao et al. implement active monitoring in a virtualized environment. They try to bridge the semantic gap between disk blocks and logic files with the help of the block tap library *blktap* [6]. However, they still allow the modification of files in security-critical directories (e.g., /etc) while only logging these modifications, thus being incapable of *preventing* potential attacks. Our active monitoring approach allows VMs to autonomously upgrade software packages in a controlled manner, thus implicitly enabling the secure and restricted modification of files in security-critical directories.

HIMA [23] provides hypervisor-based active monitoring of critical guest events and guest memory protection. However, their described approach requires considerable effort for bridging the semantic gap. In contrast, our approach is very efficient in preserving the semantic knowledge of file operation events within VMs on a high-level abstraction by utilizing the Plan 9 protocol.

Lares [7] and Xenprobe [8] place hooks in the guest VMs in order to trace syscalls. However, these hooks can be attacked and disabled from within the VM. Hence, the hypervisor is not able to reliably monitor the VMs. Our approach of relocating the guest VM's filesystem from the realm of the guest VM to the host guarantees that all file operations originating from a VM are necessarily routed through the hypervisor in order to implement reliable monitoring.

8 Conclusion

In this paper, we presented our virtualized architecture that allows for active file integrity monitoring. The key idea of our approach is to relocate a supervised VM's entire filesystem into the isolated realm of the host such that all file operations must necessarily be routed through the hypervisor. This allows for complete active monitoring and the prevention of critical filesystem events. In contrast to existing active monitoring approaches, our technique has the advantage that hooks placed inside the VMs are not prone to manipulation by malware. The reason is that disabling hooks in a VM inevitably renders the VM incapable of accessing or manipulating its own filesystem (provided by the respective hook). Another key feature of our approach is that we enable regular users of VMs to autonomously install and upgrade software packages in a secure and controlled manner, without the need of requiring the intervention of the administrator of the physical system. Finally, we securely measure all executed binaries of all VMs and store these measurements in a single, multiplexed TPM. The experimental results of our prototype implementation show the practicality of our approach.

Acknowledgements. We would like to thank our colleagues Julian Horsch and Steffen Wagner for fruitful discussions and valuable comments. This work was partly supported by the Federal Ministry of Economics and Technology (BMWi) through grant 01MD11012.

References

1. Kim, G.H., Spafford, E.H.: The design and implementation of Tripwire: A file system integrity checker. In: Proceedings of the 2nd ACM Conference on Computer and Communications Security, pp. 18–29. ACM (1994)
2. Smalley, S., Vance, C., Salamon, W.: Implementing SELinux as a Linux security module. NAI Labs Report 1, 43 (2001)
3. Garfinkel, T., Rosenblum, M.: A Virtual Machine Introspection Based Architecture for Intrusion Detection. In: Proc. Network and Distributed Systems Security Symposium, pp. 191–206 (2003)

4. Nance, K., Bishop, M., Hay, B.: Virtual machine introspection: Observation or interference? IEEE Security & Privacy 6(5), 32–37 (2008)
5. Jones, S.T., Arpaci-Dusseau, A.C., Arpaci-Dusseau, R.H.: Antfarm: Tracking processes in a virtual machine environment. In: Proceedings of the USENIX Annual Technical Conference, pp. 1–14 (2006)
6. Payne, B.D., de Carbone, M.D.P., Lee, W.: Secure and flexible monitoring of virtual machines. In: Twenty-Third Annual Computer Security Applications Conference, ACSAC 2007, pp. 385–397 (2007)
7. Payne, B.D., Carbone, M., Sharif, M., Lares, W.L.: An architecture for secure active monitoring using virtualization. In: IEEE Symposium on Security and Privacy, SP 2008, pp. 233–247. IEEE (2008)
8. Quynh, N.A., Suzaki, K.: Xenprobes, a lightweight user-space probing framework for xen virtual machine. In: USENIX Annual Technical Conference Proceedings (2007)
9. Zhao, F., Jiang, Y., Xiang, G., Jin, H., Jiang, W.: VRFPS: A Novel Virtual Machine-Based Real-time File Protection System. In: Proceedings of the 2009 Seventh ACIS International Conference on Software Engineering Research, Management and Applications, SERA 2009, Washington, DC, USA, pp. 217–224 (2009)
10. Van Hensbergen, E., Minnich, R.: Grave Robbers from outer space using 9P2000 under Linux. In: Proceedings of the Annual Conference on USENIX Annual Technical Conference, ATEC 2005, p. 45. USENIX Association, Berkeley (2005)
11. Velten, M., Stumpf, F.: Secure and Privacy-Aware Multiplexing of Hardware-Protected TPM Integrity Measurements among Virtual Machines. In: Kwon, T., Lee, M.-K., Kwon, D. (eds.) ICISC 2012. LNCS, vol. 7839, pp. 324–336. Springer, Heidelberg (2013)
12. Russell, R.: Virtio: towards a de-facto standard for virtual I/O devices. ACM SIGOPS Operating Systems Review 42(5), 95–103 (2008)
13. Trusted Platform Module, Main Specification, Level 2, Version 1.2, Revision 116 (2011), http://www.trustedcomputinggroup.org/resources/tpm_main_specification
14. Plan 9 – 9P2000.L Protocol, https://code.google.com/p/diod/w/list
15. Tool Interface Standard (TIS) – Executable and Linking Format (ELF) Specification (May 1995), http://refspecs.linuxbase.org/elf/elf.pdf
16. Sailer, R., Zhang, X., Jaeger, T., van Doorn, L.: Design and implementation of a TCG-based integrity measurement architecture. In: Proceedings of the 13th Conference on USENIX Security Symposium, SSYM 2004, vol. 13. USENIX Association, Berkeley (2004)
17. Native Linux KVM Tool, https://github.com/penberg/linux-kvm
18. Kivity, A., Kamay, Y., Laor, D., Lublin, U., Liguori, A.: kvm: the Linux virtual machine monitor. In: OLS 2007: Proceedings of the Linux Symposium, vol. 1, pp. 225–230 (June 2007)
19. Bellard, F.: QEMU, a fast and portable dynamic translator. In: Proceedings of the Annual Conference on USENIX Annual Technical Conference, ATEC 2005. USENIX Association, Berkeley (2005)
20. Wessel, S., Stumpf, F.: Page-based Runtime Integrity Protection of User and Kernel Code. In: 5th European Workshop on System Security (2012)

21. Litty, L., Lagar-Cavilla, H.A., Lie, D.: Hypervisor support for identifying covertly executing binaries. In: Proceedings of the 17th Conference on Security Symposium, SS 2008, pp. 243–258. USENIX Association, Berkeley (2008)
22. Patil, S., Kashyap, A., Sivathanu, G., Zadok, E.: I3FS: An in-kernel integrity checker and intrusion detection file system. In: Proceedings of the 18th Annual Large Installation System Administration Conference, LISA 2004 (2004)
23. Azab, A.M., Ning, P., Sezer, E.C., Zhang, X.: HIMA: A Hypervisor-Based Integrity Measurement Agent. In: ACSAC, pp. 461–470. IEEE Computer Society (2009)

Remote Policy Enforcement for Trusted Application Execution in Mobile Environments*

Fabio Martinelli[2], Ilaria Matteucci[2],
Andrea Saracino[1,2], and Daniele Sgandurra[2]

[1] Dipartimento di Ingegneria dell'Informazione,
Università di Pisa, Pisa, Italy
name.surname@iet.unipi.it
[2] Istituto di Informatica e Telematica,
Consiglio Nazionale delle Ricerche, Pisa, Italy
name.surname@iit.cnr.it

Abstract. Both in the cloud and mobile environments, a large number of online services is daily accessed through smartphones and tablets. Since several security, safety and trust concerns may arise when using these services, providers may require a usage policy to be enforced on the devices while accessing these services. This kind of policy enforcements enables service providers to have assurance that remote devices are in an acceptable state when using the provided service, according to their terms and conditions.

In this paper, we propose a framework which allows service providers to have assurance about the enforcement of some functional policies directly on the device. The proposed framework inserts an *enforcer* into the client's device, which is responsible for enforcing the provider's policy to abide by the terms and conditions of the service. To assure the integrity of the enforcer and of the policy, the framework exploits Trusted Computing techniques to remotely attest the enforcer's measurements. Preliminary experiments and a first prototype implementation for Android-based smartphones suggest that the approach is both viable and effective.

1 Introduction

Mobile devices are used to access a large number of online services, such as e-banking, multimedia streaming, location services, videogames and social networking. Since some security and safety concerns may be raised when using these online services, providers may be willing to have some assurance that, when using them, devices are in a well-know, and acceptable, state. As an example, it is safe if no key-logging software is active on the device during an e-bank transaction, due to the sensitive data exchanged. Hence, a safe usage of online services may require the definition of specific behaviors

---

* The research leading to these results has received funding from the EU Seventh Framework Programme (FP7/2007-2013) under grant n. 256980 (NESSoS), n. 257930 (Aniketos), from PRIN Security Horizons funded by MIUR with D.D. 23.10.2012 n. 719, and EIT ICT Labs activity 13077.

R. Bloem and P. Lipp (Eds.): INTRUST 2013, LNCS 8292, pp. 70–84, 2013.

for the remote clients. These behaviors forbid actions that are incompatible with the service itself.

The set of the correct expected behaviors defined by a provider constitutes a *provider policy*. The definition and enforcement of a policy should provide a safe service usage both from the user and provider point of view and may also be part of an agreement on the service conditions between the user and the provider. In fact, in this scenario, the provider may grant a determined Quality of Service (QoS) only if the user behavior is compliant with a certain specification. For example, a video-streaming provider may grant the streaming of high definition videos with a negligible latency, assuming that the available bandwidth is higher than a predefined threshold. However, supposing that the user is filling the bandwidth using other network-exhausting programs (e.g., through torrent, download manager, etc.), the QoS of the agreement cannot be provided. The monitoring of the effective behaviors, to discover if there are policy violations, can be hard to implement in real-scenarios since (i) provider policies may concern behaviors of third-party applications, OS, users or other components that are not controlled by the provider itself; (ii) it may be deceived by malicious applications installed on a device.

To overcome these issues, we propose a provider policy enforcement framework based upon remote attestation. The proposed framework allows providers to have assurance that service policies are enforced by remote devices when using their services. To this end, policy compliance is applied by a global enforcer running on the device, which monitors all the security-relevant events on a mobile device. The enforcer periodically submits policy reports to the service provider. To ensure that both the enforcer and the policies have not been compromised, or faked, the framework exploits a Trusted Platform Module (TPM) on the device to build a chain-of-trust. In this way, the provider can have assurance that, when enforcing the policy, the remote device is in a trusted state.

Contributions. The contributions of the paper are multifold and include the following:

- we propose a remote measurement framework to provide assurance to service providers about the enforcement of policies on remote devices when accessing their services;
- we discuss the format of the policy to be globally enforced on remote devices: the policy is sealed with the application, and it specifies acceptable behaviors that are compliant with the terms of service;
- we provide a protocol for both attesting the initial state of the device and to alert the provider in case of policy violations;
- we discuss the first prototype implementation and the first results.

Outline of the Paper. The paper is organized as follows. Section 2 recalls some background notions related to the Trusted Computing Platform and to the Android Framework. In Sect. 3 we describe in detail the architecture of the proposed framework. Section 4 presents the first prototype of the framework along with some examples of the policies instantiated to some real use cases. Section 5 discusses some related works while Sect. 6 concludes by proposing further extensions.

2   Background

In this section we recall some notions about Trusted Computing, Android system, and the main components requested to build a remote attestation service.

2.1   Trusted Computing

One prominent framework of integrity measurement is promoted by the Trusted Computing Group (TCG), which is an industry consortium that defines specifications for hardware and software components [1]. The standard TCG measurement basically requires the computation of SHA-1 cryptographic hash of critical software components as soon as they are loaded into the system. The TCG guidance for measurement includes the Trusted Platform Module (TPM) as a hardware device to securely store and report measurement values through SHA-1 hash. This architecture provides a good framework for determining the integrity during software initialization. Since the TCG framework is pretty complex, we detail here some of its main components:

- RTM (Root-of-Trust for Measurement) is a on-device chip capable of performing reliable integrity measurements. This is the root of the chain of transitive trust.
- CRTM (Core Root-of-Trust for Measurement) is the small set of instructions that are executed by the platform when it acts as the RTM.
- RTS (Root-of-Trust for Storage) is the part of the framework responsible for maintaining a not-modifiable summary of values of integrity digests and the sequence of digests.
- RTR (Root-of-Trust for Reporting) is the part of the framework that reliably reports information held by the RTS.
- PCR (Platform Configuration Register) are the set of physical, and tamper-proof, registers containing a digest of integrity digests.
- TPM (Trusted Platform Module) is used to implement all the functions defined in the TCG specification and includes the set of Root-of-Trust with shielded locations and protected capabilities.
- TSS (TPM Software Stack) is a library used by higher-level services that facilitates the use of the TPM.

In the following, we describe in more detail the TPM functionalities.

TPM and MTM. The TPM acts as a root-of-trust in the process that builds and configures the software environments and it ensures that a system has loaded its software properly. Moreover, it protects secrets such as asymmetric and symmetric keys. The TPM has a set of registers that are protected from the system software. The TPM implements two operations on each register content: `extend` and `quote`. The `extend` operation takes a value V as input and computes the SHA-1 hash of the current register content and V. This function is used to compute and store the hash of new values. Instead, in a `quote` operation, the TPM generates a message with the register contents and signs it with a private key protected by the TPM.

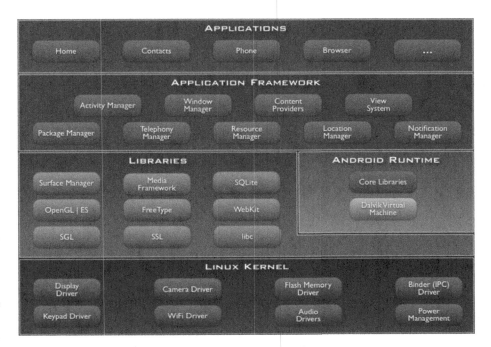

Fig. 1. Android Architecture (From [2])

The Mobile Trusted Module (MTM) is both a security device and an approved TCG specification [3] [4] for mobile devices. The specification for mobile devices differs from TPM specifications by introducing the concept of secure boot and by specifying the implementation of the MTM as a functionality rather than as a physical implementation in hardware and, finally, by taking into account the support of several coexisting MTMs in the same device. As an example, some of these may enforce discretionary policies (e.g.., MTMs exposed to user applications) whereas others may enforce mandatory security policies(e.g., the device manufacturer MTM).

2.2 Android

Android is an open source Operating System (OS) designed for mobile devices, such as smartphones and tablets, which currently has the largest share of the mobile device market. Android is a complex framework divided in several functional blocks and levels (Figure 1). The lowest level is a Linux kernel, cross-compiled through a toolchain, in order to run on mobile device architectures, i.e. ARM processors. Some binaries that can be commonly found on desktop distributions have been removed, to produce a lighter kernel more suitable to mobile devices. Applications (*apps*) run at higher level (Application Level) in a sandboxed environment. Each application runs in a virtual machine called *Dalvik Virtual Machine (DVM)*, which is a Java Virtual Machine optimized to run on mobile devices. Every instance of the DVM is handled as a different Linux user, with its own storage and virtual memory space. This ensures application isolation,

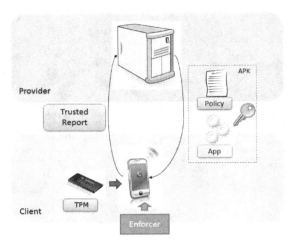

Fig. 2. Client-Provider Architecture

i.e. each application runs in its sandbox and cannot interfere with other running or idle applications.

Both the application framework and the libraries level offer a large number of APIs to allow applications to interact with device components and kernel functions. The number of applications available for Android systems is continuously growing. The official online market for applications, i.e., Google Play, distributes more than 700K apps. Several applications require Internet access to provide a service and are based on a classical client-server paradigm, where the server provides a service to all the clients (mobile devices) requesting it.

3   Architecture

This section describes the architecture of the proposed framework, and it specifies the components that have to be ported on Android systems. The architecture is composed of two main parts: the client-side, i.e. the on-device enforcement mechanism, and the provider-side part, i.e. the provider policy specification. A high-level view of the system is shown in Fig. 2.

We first start by describing some real-world use cases to show the viability and the benefits of the proposed architecture.

Secure Driving. Consider a street navigation software, e.g. `Google Maps`, which allows users, e.g. in cars, to continuously receive route directions while driving. The provider of such a software may require that while driving texting and app-browsing are forbidden to avoid possible distractions while driving that may pose serious risks to the safety of the driver[1]. In fact, if the application is used, this means that the user may be

---

[1] This could be based upon the speed of the user/device, e.g. to avoid forbidding messaging apps while walking.

in a potential dangerous situation. Hence, an example of a remote policy enforcement is to block all the operations that require a user manual interaction to avoid possible distractions while driving.

Flight Mode. Usually, while on board of a plane passengers are asked to keep their mobile phones in Flight Mode (radio interface down) for the entire duration of the flight, as the radio interface may interfere with the airplane system. In such a situation, the airline company may enable users to download an application that constantly updates their phones through Wi-Fi on the current plane position[2], weather condition of the final destination, delay if any. In such a scenario, a policy to be enforced on the device is to disable the telephony radio interface and only allow Wi-Fi to access on-board services while flying.

Real Location. The provider of a location-based service may require that no services of location obfuscation are active on the device. Location-based services provide a reliable service only if the given location is correct. In such a scenario, a policy to be locally enforced on the device may be based on a black-list of applications, known to obfuscate the location, that cannot run on the device while the location-based service is active

Game Fairness. Online games are known to be populated by unfair players that try to cheat to gain more popularity / points or simply to provide denial of service both to the service provider and other players. As an example, users may exploit some applications to simulate a heavy network latency, slowing the reaction of their adversaries. In this scenario, a game-provider would like to forbid the usage of cheating applications when the user is playing its online video-game.

3.1   Provider-Side Architecture

Service providers may require to have some assurance that, when using their online services, remote devices are in a well-known, and acceptable, state. Hence, in the proposed framework, users access online services through apps developed and distributed by the provider itself that are shipped together with a policy to be enforced. A *policy* is a formal complete specification of the acceptable security-relevant behavior allowed to applications executed on the platform [5]. Policies may also concern user or OS behaviors and may be expressed using (i) several formalisms, such as formal specification languages [6], (ii) high-level or natural language, or (iii) execution graphs. To enforce a policy, the behaviors that are of interest should be constantly monitored, by verifying that they match the ones described in the policy, otherwise they should be forbidden.

Policy Format. Each provider policy is written in eXtensible Markup Language (XML) using a nested tag structure to specify allowed and disallowed actions. In the current implementation the full list of XML tags enables control on the following elements:

- Blacklist and whitelist of installed or running applications.
- Usage of network interfaces, such as data connection, Wi-Fi, Bluetooth and NFC.

---

[2] E.g., on Windows Phone devices, during flight mode it is possible to enable Wi-Fi.

Table 1. Policy Specification

```
<policy default_reaction={deny, report, lower_trust}>
<networking>
      <wifi reaction={deny, report, lower_trust}> {enabled,disabled} </wifi>
      <radio reaction={deny, report, lower_trust}> {enabled,disabled} </radio>
      <bluetooth reaction={deny, report, lower_trust}> {enabled,disabled} </
          bluetooth>
      <nfc reaction={deny, report, lower_trust}> {enabled,disabled} </nfc>
</networking>
<telephony>
      <call reaction={deny, report, lower_trust} time_per_day=[1,1440]
          number_per_day=[1,inf] direction={outgoing, incoming}> {enabled,
          disabled} </call>
      <sms reaction={deny, report, lower_trust} number_per_day=[1,inf] direction={
          outgoing, incoming}> {enabled,disabled} </sms>
      <mms reaction={deny, report, lower_trust} number_per_day=[1,inf] direction={
          outgoing, incoming}> {enabled,disabled} </mms>
</telephony>
<location>
      <gps reaction={deny, report, lower_trust} time_per_day=[1,1440]> {enabled,
          disabled} </gps>
      <cell_location reaction={deny, report, lower_trust}> {enabled,disabled} </
          cell_location>
      <ip_location reaction={deny, report, lower_trust}> {enabled,disabled} </
          ip_location>
</location>
<input>
      <touchscreen reaction={deny, report, lower_trust}> {enabled,disabled} </
          touchscreen>
      <keyboard reaction={deny, report, lower_trust}> {enabled,disabled} </
          keyboard>
      <side_button reaction={deny, report, lower_trust}> {enabled,disabled} </
          side_button>
      <voice_input reaction={deny, report, lower_trust}> {enabled,disabled} </
          voice_input>
</input>
<output>
      <ringtone reaction={deny, report, lower_trust}> {enabled,disabled} </
          ringtone>
      <speakerphone reaction={deny, report, lower_trust}> {enabled,disabled} </
          speakerphone>
</output>
<app_running>
      <app1 package_name={package_name1}> {enabled,disabled} </app1>
      <app2 package_name={package_name2}> {enabled,disabled} </app2>
      ...
      <appn package_name={package_name1}> {enabled,disabled} </appn>
</app_running>
<app_installed>
      <app1 package_name={package_name1}> {enabled,disabled} </app1>
      <app2 package_name={package_name2}> {enabled,disabled} </app2>
      ...
      <appn package_name={package_name1}> {enabled,disabled} </appn>
</app_installed>
</policy>
```

- Enabled input mechanisms, e.g. touch-screen, physical keyboard, voice commands, etc.
- Outgoing voice traffic, SMS/MMS messages, raw data through network interfaces.
- Black list and white list of contacts.
- Usage of location providers.

The full policy specification language is described in Table 1. The policy can also be extended by adding new XML tags to control more smartphone elements. Each XML tag specifies the policy for a critical device component using a nested structure. The possible value for each tag is either `enabled` or `disabled`, where `disabled` means that the component cannot be used. Through attributes it is possible to define finer grained policies. By default each component is enabled. The attribute `default_reaction` of the policy tag specifies the default reaction for policy violations. This reaction can be customized for each component using the `reaction` attribute of each policy subtag. The criticality order is, from the less critical to the most critical: `lower_trust`, `report`, `deny`.

To implement these specifications on Android devices, the framework needs to update the `AndroidManifest.xml` file. In Android, every application comes in the form of an APK file. Android application package file (APK) is the file format used to distribute and install application software. Every APK must have an `AndroidManifest.xml` file in its root directory. The manifest presents essential information about the application components and security relevant authorization that the application requires to work correctly. Since the policy is part of the application (APK), we have decided to express the policy in XML so to be included in the `AndroidManifest.xml` file. This file is bound to the application by means of digital signature, to ensure the integrity of both application and policy. When installing the application, the user accepts the provider policy, which will be enforced on the device.

3.2 Client-Side Architecture

In this section we detail the on-device components required to support the integrity measurement/reporting and policy enforcement.

Enforcer. The enforcer is a multi-layer component, which monitors the action performed on the device, and enforces the provider policy. In the current implementation, the monitoring is performed both at application-level and kernel-level, but this component can be extended to enforce policies and monitor behaviors at any level. When the enforcer detects a behavior that is non-compliant with a policy, the enforcer executes a *reaction*, which is an action specified in a policy to react to a performed misbehavior. Examples of reactions are:

- *Deny*: the misbehavior is blocked before it takes place;
- *Report*: the provider is notified about the non-compliance of the device/application with the policy;
- *Trust Lowering*: the trust level of the client is lowered. Different strategies may be applied towards clients with low trust levels.

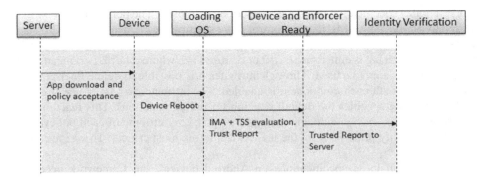

Fig. 3. Remote Attestation Protocol

In the current prototype, the enforcer has been implemented by modifying the system at the application level and inserting a Linux module at kernel-level. The part of the enforcement at application level monitors the device interfaces activities, like GPS, Wi-Fi, Bluetooth and NFC. This component also controls and handles the events of outgoing and incoming phone calls and SMS/MMS messages. The kernel module tracks all the running processes and is responsible of stopping (or reporting, or lowering the trust level of, according to the policy) the applications that violate a policy.

Trusted Policy Enforcement. Integrity of the client-side architecture is assured through usage of Trusted Computing. The Trusted Computing building blocks that have to be included on the Android platform have been described in [16], and are the following: a Root-of-Trust for Measurement (RTM), a Root-of-Trust for Storage and Reporting (RTS/RTR) and a Static Chain of Trust (SCoT). To build the Chain-of-Trust, the Linux kernel is enhanced by including the Integrity Measurement Architecture (IMA). The enforcer exploits a minimal TSS implementation for PCR `extend` operations, to allow its measurement functions to communicate the results to the TPM, and for PCR `quote` to enable the trustworthy reporting of the stored value registers of the PCR to the remote provider.

The framework requires a verification of the initial device integrity through a set of measurements on its configuration, which includes a set of hash computations of the code of its kernel and of the running applications. The root-of-trust is rooted to the physical platform TPM. Hence, to measure the initial integrity of the device, starting with the TPM, the following steps are required. Firstly, the TPM applies a set of measurements on the boot-loader, so that from now on, all the steps can be measured from boot to kernel loading and its modules. Attestation requires that the measurements of the device are certified by the keys stored in the TPM and that the provider can establish trust in the device's integrity based upon these measurements. By computing the hash of the running software, signed by the private key of the TPM, the provider can be assured of the trustworthiness of the data received. Then, further integrity measurements are performed by IMA, ported for Android, which communicates with the TPM to safely measure, and store the results of, all the executables loaded on the device as well as the Dalvik VM, run-time libraries and the enforcer.

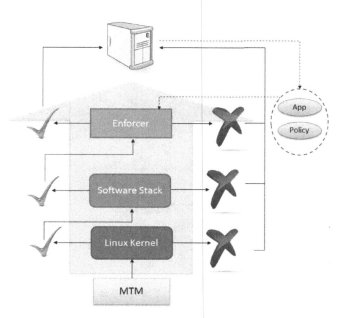

Fig. 4. Trusted Chain

These steps establish the first chain-of-trust up to the Dalvik VM and the enforcer. Then, the enforcer is responsible for ensuring that the chain-of-trust reaches the considered application. To this end, the enforcer continuously monitors the device status according to the received policy, i.e. by forbidding any unacceptable behavior and/or by reporting the misbehavior to the service provider. Once the attestation tokens (PCR quote and measurements logs) are received by the service provider, which acts as a challenger, the service provider needs to verify the trustworthiness, and policy compliance, of the remote device. This basically means to validate the digital signature on the quotes. This step is necessary to verify that a genuine TPM vouches for the measurements logs that, hence, are not fake and unmodified. To verify this, the service provider requires the public portion of Attestation Identity Key (AIK), which is issued using by a certification authority. The AIK is used for platform authentication, platform attestation and certification of keys. The whole chain-of-trust of the proposed framework is depicted in Fig. 4.

4   Preliminary Tests

This section reports a brief description of the current implementation on Android devices and presents some experiments with some example policies.

4.1   Current Prototype

In the current prototype, since no Android devices include a MTM module, some MTM emulators exist that implement their functionalities in software. Since we only need few

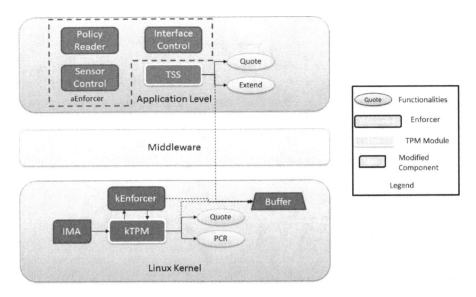

Fig. 5. On-Device Framework Architecture

of these functionalities, we have implemented a simple MTM emulator that provides TPM quote and protected storage only as a kernel module, called *kTPM*. The functions exported by kTPM can be called either by the kernel itself, through the IMA (modified to call these functions, i.e. the communication with the TPM is emulated through these two functions) and the enforcer, which includes the TSS (Trusted Software Stack) that communicates directly with kTPM. This communication is implemented by a protocol on a shared buffer in the /proc/ directory, where basically the TSS writes the requested action and the parameters, then it loops until results are written by the kTPM.

As shown in Fig. 5, the enforcer is composed of several components, divided in two parts. The first part is the enforcer at the application-level (*aEnforcer*), and the second one at the kernel-level (*kEnforcer*). The *aEnforcer* includes the *policyReader*, which takes as input the policy in XML format. The *aEnforcer* also includes the *sensorController* and *interfaceController*, which are used to monitor and control the activities of the various sensors and network interface. As an example, it can shutdown interfaces on request if the policy requests so. Finally, the *aEnforcer* also includes the minimal TSS implementation to directly communicate with kTPM.

The kernel-level part of the enforcer, i.e. the *kEnforcer*, communicates bidirectionally with the application-part through the /proc/kenf file. As an example of policy enforcement, the *kEnforcer* may kill all the processes related to an application that violates a policy.

4.2   Experimentations

We have tested the prototype in all the use-cases described in Sect. 3 by simulating the environment. To this end, we first have coded four simple applications that emulate the functionalities requested by each scenario, e.g. a simple game for the Game Fairness scenario and the corresponding policy. The provider is emulated through a simple PHP server that sends the APK file of the tested applications with the manifest file including the policy and communicates with the emulator and then listens for communications through an exported interface of a Web Service.

In all of the four tests, the policy has been correctly enforced: as an example, as soon as an action violates the policy, the application has been killed by the the *kEnforcer* or the *aEnforcer* has reported the misbehavior to the server/provider. In the following, we report all the XML policies used in the tests.

Table 2. Policy Specification of Secure Driving Use-Case

```
<policy default_reaction="deny">
  <telephony>
    <call direction="outgoing">disabled</call>
    <sms direction="outgoing">disabled</sms>
    <mms direction="outgoing">disabled</mms>
  </telephony>
  <input>
    <touchscreen>disabled</touchscreen>
    <keyboard>disabled</keyboard>
    <side_button>disabled</side_button>
  </input>
</policy>
```

Secure Driving. This policy is active only when the navigation mode of the software is active, which is after the user has chosen the destination and is driving. To avoid that the user get distracted by the smartphone, all interaction that require an active user interaction have been disabled. The user can only interact with the device using voice controls. The full policy is described in Table 2.

Table 3. Policy Specification of Flight Mode Use-Case

```
<policy default_reaction="report">
  <networking>
    <radio>disabled</radio>
  </networking>
  <app_installed>
    <app_1 package_name="com.myflightcompany.surfandfly">enabled</app_1>
  </app_installed>
</policy>
```

Flight Mode. This policy mandates that the user keeps the radio interface of her phone disabled during flight. This is a safety requirement that should be enforced when the user is on-board. The policy is violated if the user enables the radio interface or uninstall the application, e.g. trying to avoid the policy enforcement. In both cases, the enforcement strategy is *report* so that the server, together with the cabin crew of the airplane, will know if the policy has been violated and who is violating the policy. The full policy is described in Table 3.

Table 4. Policy Specification of Game Fairness and Real Location Use-Cases

```
<policy default_reaction="deny">
  <app_running>
    <app_1 package_name="com.myfakelocator.fakelocator">disabled</app_1>
  </app_running>
</policy>
```

Real Location and Game Fairness. This policy forbids programs able to forge the user location to run while the provider location service is running. Similarly, a list of known cheating programs for online videogames may be blacklisted using the same technique. The full policy is described in Table 4.

5   Related Work

The design and implementation of Integrity Measurement Architecture (IMA), a secure integrity measurement system for Linux, is discussed in [8]. IMA enables automatic measurement of all software, such as program, libraries, and kernel modules, and it can also be used to measure static data files when specified by the software. [9] discusses an access control architecture that enables corporations to verify the integrity of a remote client and establish trust into its ability to enforce a security policy before allowing the client to access corporate Intranet services. *Property based attestation* [10] [11] is a framework to describe the behavior of the platform to be attested with respect to security-related requirements. As an example, a property may state that a platform has built-in mechanisms to conform to the privacy laws, or that it strictly separates processes from each other. With property attestation, a verifier is securely assured of security properties of the execution environment of the verified platform without receiving detailed configuration data. *Semantic integrity* [12] is a measurement approach targeting the dynamic state of the software during execution and, therefore, providing fresh measurement results. This approach can provide increased flexibility for the challenger, because the integrity monitor can examine the current state of a system to detect semantic integrity violations. Prima [13] is an extension of the Linux IMA system, that measures information flow integrity and can be verified by remote parties. [14] presents a framework to protect a mobile application at run-time through the use of TCG technologies. Application developers define an application policy that is enforced locally on the device. Examples of such policies are controlling which users can run the applications or what kind of results they can observe. A framework for remote attestation, implemented on the Android platform is presented in [15]. However, the presented framework is only used to verify the device integrity, ensuring that no unknown software is running on the device. [16] proposes an attestation approach for Android smartphones that integrates TCG and the Android's permission system, in particular by attesting the permissions used by the installed applications to a remote party at run-time. The authors of [17] propose a malware prevention architecture for smartphones that exploits applications signatures, process authentication and verification. The proposed framework allows a smartphone to run only trusted applications, e.g., signed applications, and those that are not modified. The trust of an application is a function of the application signature and MTM and is propagated through the processes through process authentication. Differently from the previous approach, the framework proposed in this paper is the first one that exploits Trusted Computing to verify the remote enforcement of provider policies. Finally, Mobile device management (MDM) [18] is a way to monitor and manage mobile devices deployed across mobile operators, enterprises by distributing applications, data and configuration settings over-the-air.

6   Conclusion and Future Work

In this paper we have presented a policy enforcement system for Android applications that access online services. Policies are given by service providers, to enforce both safety and security for the device and for the user. Policy enforcement is assured through an enforcement module included in the Android system and a Trusted Computing Platform, which ensures the integrity of reports sent to the server. We have presented a policy specification formalism that exploits XML language and the modification requested to include our system on Android devices. The proposed approach enables the definition and enforcement of provider policies, which users have to accept to access the service. The current implementation exploits an emulated MTM to implement the functions of Trusted Computing, which are requested to assure authenticity and integrity of the reported device status.

A first future extension of this work consists in including our framework on mobile devices with a real MTM. To the best of our knowledge, currently there are no devices that include both the MTM and the Android OS. Afterward we are planning to test our framework in an enterprise environment that uses the Bring Your Own Device paradigm with employers, by considering finer grained policies that takes in account context information. Finally, we plan to reduce the number of modifications requested to a standard device by requiring the provider to include into a single bundle both the application and the enforcer, along with the policy.

References

1. Pearson, S.: Trusted Computing Platforms, the Next Security Solution. Trusted Computing Group Administration, Beaverton (2002)
2. Wikipedia: Android operating system (2013),
   http://en.wikipedia.org/wiki/Android_(operating_system)
3. Trusted Computing Group: Mobile phone work group mobile trusted module specification, version 1.0, revision 7.02 (2013)
4. Trusted Computing Group: Mobile phone work group mobile reference architecture (2013)
5. Greci, P., Martinelli, F., Matteucci, I.: A framework for contract-policy matching based on symbolic simulations for securing mobile device application. In: Margaria, T., Steffen, B. (eds.) ISoLA 2008. CCIS, vol. 17, pp. 221–236. Springer, Heidelberg (2008)
6. Aktug, I., Naliuka, K.: Conspec – a formal language for policy specification. Electron. Notes Theor. Comput. Sci. 197(1), 45–58 (2008)

7. Bente, I., Dreo, G., Hellmann, B., Heuser, S., Vieweg, J., Von Helden, J., Westhuis, J.: Towards permission-based attestation for the android platform. In: McCune, J.M., Balacheff, B., Perrig, A., Sadeghi, A.-R., Sasse, A., Beres, Y. (eds.) TRUST 2011. LNCS, vol. 6740, pp. 108–115. Springer, Heidelberg (2011)

8. Sailer, R., Zhang, X., Jaeger, T.: Design and implementation of a TCG-based integrity measurement architecture. In: Proceedings of the 13th Conference on USENIX Security Symposium, vol. 13, p. 16 (2004)

9. Sailer, R., Jaeger, T., Zhang, X., van Doorn, L.: Attestation-based policy enforcement for remote access. In: CCS 2004: Proceedings of the 11th ACM Conference on Computer and Communications Security, pp. 308–317. ACM, New York (2004)

10. Sadeghi, A.R., Stüble, C.: Property-based attestation for computing platforms: caring about properties, not mechanisms. In: NSPW 2004: Proceedings of the 2004 Workshop on New Security Paradigms, pp. 67–77. ACM, New York (2004)

11. Chen, L., Landfermann, R., Löhr, H., Rohe, M., Sadeghi, A., Stüble, C.: A protocol for property-based attestation. In: Proceedings of the First ACM Workshop on Scalable Trusted Computing, pp. 7–16. ACM, New York (2006)

12. Petroni Jr., N., Fraser, T., Walters, A., Arbaugh, W.: An Architecture for Specification-Based Detection of Semantic Integrity Violations in Kernel Dynamic Data. In: Proc. of the 15th USENIX Security Symposium (2006)

13. Jaeger, T., Sailer, R., Shankar, U.: PRIMA: policy-reduced integrity measurement architecture. In: Proceedings of the Eleventh ACM Symposium on Access Control Models and Technologies, pp. 19–28. ACM, New York (2006)

14. Zhang, X., Parisi-Presicce, F., Sandhu, R.: Towards remote policy enforcement for runtime protection of mobile code using trusted computing. In: Yoshiura, H., Sakurai, K., Rannenberg, K., Murayama, Y., Kawamura, S. (eds.) IWSEC 2006. LNCS, vol. 4266, pp. 179–195. Springer, Heidelberg (2006)

15. Nauman, M., Khan, S., Zhang, X., Seifert, J.-P.: Beyond kernel-level integrity measurement: Enabling remote attestation for the android platform. In: Acquisti, A., Smith, S.W., Sadeghi, A.-R. (eds.) TRUST 2010. LNCS, vol. 6101, pp. 1–15. Springer, Heidelberg (2010)

16. Bente, I., Dreo, G., Hellmann, B., Heuser, S., Vieweg, J., Von Helden, J., Westhuis, J.: Towards permission-based attestation for the android platform. In: McCune, J.M., Balacheff, B., Perrig, A., Sadeghi, A.-R., Sasse, A., Beres, Y. (eds.) TRUST 2011. LNCS, vol. 6740, pp. 108–115. Springer, Heidelberg (2011)

17. Ugus, O., Westhoff, D.: An mtm based watchdog for malware famishment in smartphones. In: Eichler, G., Küpper, A., Schau, V., Fouchal, H., Unger, H. (eds.) IICS. LNI, vol. P-186, pp. 251–262. GI (2011)

18. Joseph, A.: Mobile device management-brave new horizon or basic plumbing? (2013), http://www.devicemanagement.org/content/view/20754/152/

Towards Policy Engineering for Attribute-Based Access Control*

Leanid Krautsevich, Aliaksandr Lazouski,
Fabio Martinelli, and Artsiom Yautsiukhin

Istituto di Informatica e Telematica Consiglio Nazionale delle Ricerche
name.surname@iit.cnr.it

Abstract. Attribute-based Access Control (ABAC) was recently proposed as a general model which is able to capture the main existing access control models. This paper discusses the problems of configuring ABAC and engineering access policies. We question how to design attributes, how to assign attributes to subjects, objects, actions, and how to formulate access policies which bind subjects to objects and actions via attributes.

Inspired by the role mining problem in Role-based Access Control, in this paper we propose the first attempt to formalise ABAC in a matrix form and define formally a problem of access policy engineering. Our approach is based on the XACML standard to be more practical.

Keywords: ABAC, policy engineering, access control, attributes, attribute mining problem (AMP), role mining.

1 Introduction

Attribute-based Access Control (ABAC) [1] was recently proposed as a general model which is able to capture the main existing access control models, like Discretionary Access Control (DAC), Mandatory Access Control (MAC), and Role-based Access Control (RBAC). The core components of ABAC are attributes assigned to all entities, e.g., subjects, objects, actions. Access policies define conditions (predicates over attributes) when access requests are permitted. Although ABAC provides a rich flexibility in defining access policies, there are a lot of challenges regarding a conceptual and formal definition of the model.

This paper discusses problems of configuring ABAC and engineering access policies. We question how to design attributes, how to assign attributes to subjects, objects, actions, and how to formulate access policies which bind subjects to objects and actions via attributes. To the best of our knowledge, currently there is not even a formal definition of these problems for ABAC neither solutions. We see a role mining in RBAC [2] as the most relevant problem which might be extrapolated and used to address similar problems of ABAC.

---

* This work was partly supported by EU-FP7-ICT NESSoS (256980) and PRIN Security Horizons funded by MIUR with D.D. 23.10.2012 n. 719, and EIT ICT Labs activity 13083.

R. Bloem and P. Lipp (Eds.): INTRUST 2013, LNCS 8292, pp. 85–102, 2013.

Role mining, introduced in 2003 [3], gained a lot of attention in last years and a large number of different approaches to the problem were proposed [4–6]. Role mining is generally considered as the automatic creation of roles, assignment of subjects to roles and roles to permissions (object-action pairs). Frank et al. [2] specify three aspects of a role mining problem: (i) a formal definition, (ii) an algorithm, and (iii) quality measures of the algorithm.

It is convenient to use matrices for defining the role-mining problems formally [4, 2, 6]. Matrices help to capture relations between subjects and permissions (**UPA**), subjects and roles (**UA**), and roles and permissions (**PA**). Operations on matrices allow expressing the required relations (e.g., $\mathbf{UPA} = \mathbf{UA} \times \mathbf{PA}$) and perform simplifications, if necessary.

Inspired by the role mining problem, in this paper we propose the first attempt to formalise ABAC in a matrix form and define formally a problem of engineering access policies. Our approach is based on XACML model, an open standard of ABAC proposed by OASIS [7] and widely used in industry and research. We define only the most general problem, and leave the space for further detailed elaboration of the problem for future research, when concrete scenarios are to be considered. We only propose a definition of the problem, and leave possible algorithms and their quality measurements for the future work. We show that the role mining problem is a specific case of policy engineering problem.

The paper is structured as follows. In Section 2 we provide a simple formalisation of ABAC model, based on XACML. Section 3 contains the basics for multidimensional matrix used for our model. We provide a matrix form of ABAC formalisation in Section 4. In Section 5 the policy engineering problem for ABAC is defined and exemplified for RBAC case. Finally, we provide discussion (Section 6), related work (Section 7), and conclusions (Section 8).

2   General ABAC Model

We recall important notions relevant to the ABAC model. Currently, there is not a formal definition of the general ABAC model. However, the first steps towards definition were done by Jin et al. [1] where the authors presented ABAC_α model. ABAC_α is developed to include existing models for access control such as DAC, MAC, and RBAC. Moreover, there is an OASIS standard XACML [7] that defines a language for access control policies for ABAC. Jin et al. [1] focus on the basic, minimal features of ABAC, when the XACML standard is ready for a practical use. In this paper we formalise the core ABAC features close to the XACML standard to make our approach closer to practice. Naturally, we are not able to capture all features of XACML. In the paper we focus on attribute assignment, rules definition, and simple policy decision making. Moreover, we operate with four possible decisions used in XACML. We leave formalisation of policies for the future work.

The essential goal of any access control model is to guarantee that only legitimate subjects have permission to access objects. Following XACML, suppose there is a set S of subjects $s \in S$, a set O of objects $o \in O$, a set Act of possible actions $act \in Act$ (e.g., "read"). We also may add environment to the model, but skip this part for simplicity. We define a set of all entities in the system as $E = S \cup O \cup Act$. We assume an attribute as a function $ATTR$ which assigns a value to an entity $e \in E$ such that:

$$ATTR : E \mapsto D \tag{1}$$

where D is a finite set of values, i.e., the domain of the attribute. For example, an attribute function mapping $S \mapsto \mathbb{N}$ may specify the age of the subject.

The set of rules maps attributes into one of four possible outcomes:

$$RULE : \bigotimes_{\forall i_a = 1}^{n} (D_{i_a}) \mapsto \{\bot, \top, \boxtimes, \varnothing\} \tag{2}$$

where by $\bigotimes_{\forall i_a = 1}^{n}$ we mean, that a $RULE$ function requires n attribute values of entities. It is important to note, that to identify the used value precisely we need to specify a triple: the entity (to which the attribute belongs to), the attribute (we consider), and the value. In Equation 2 the information about the entity and the attribute is present only implicitly, but in the following we will need to specify the triple explicitly. Note, that a rule does not bind a value to a specific entity when it speaks about the subject, object, or action of a request. We say that an attribute is *bound* by a rule if the rule states exactly to which entity the attribute belongs to. For example, consider the following rule "*access is allowed only if user John is on vacations*". Here we know, that the value "is on vacation" of "current work status" attribute must belong to John. Consider a rule "*access is allowed only if the subject has an e-mail from iit.cnr.it domain*". Here we know that the attribute "e-mail" belongs to a subject, but we do not know in advance who the subject is. Thus, in the first example we have a bound (to a specific entity) attribute, when in the second case we speak about a *free* attribute.

The result of the $RULE$ function is one of four possible values of domain $\Re = \{\bot, \top, \boxtimes, \varnothing\}$, where $\top$ means positive result (e.g., allow access), $\bot$ means negative result (deny access), $\boxtimes$ means undefined result (e.g., caused by division by zero), and $\varnothing$ means not available or not applicable result. Rules are further aggregated in policies (and further in policy sets) in XACML, but we skip this part in our initial model.

Finally, a Policy Decision Point (PDP) should consider all rules (policies and policy sets in the original XACML standard) and provide the final decision. In short PDP collects all authorisation decisions provided by the rules and returns "permit" if at least one rule returns "permit" decision, and "deny" otherwise.

$$PDP : \bigotimes_{\forall i_r = 1}^{n_r} (\Re_{i_r}) \mapsto \Re \tag{3}$$

Ideally, the result of the PDP should be either $\top$ or $\bot$, but $\boxtimes$ and $\varnothing$ are also possible and leave the decision for Policy Enforcement Point.

Since matrix form has proven to be convenient for solving the role mining problem, we aim for a similar matrix form for ABAC model. Indeed, the input information for the attribute mining problem is simply the number of triples (direct access control assignments): subject-object-actions, which were allowed (or denied) in the latest period of time. Such information is a three-dimensional matrix with dimensions denoting subjects, objects, and actions. Therefore, the matrix form should explicitly link all functions defined in the current section and result in direct access control assignments. Such assignments explicitly show whether a user can perform an action on an object. Finally, using such form we will be able to define the attribute mining problem.

3   Mathematical Basis

Before we will be able to define our model we would like to specify the mathematical basis for our model. In the paper we use multidimensional matrices, i.e., the matrices which may have an arbitrary number of dimensions. Multidimensional matrices are usually considered as tensors. In contrast, we build our theory using Multidimensional Matrix Mathematics proposed by Solo [8]. This mathematics adopts all operations from tensor analysis and keeps it simple and close to the classical (2-dimensional) matrix mathematics.

In the paper we denote matrixes with bold capital capital letters e.g., $\mathbf{A}$ (when functions are denoted with capital letters not in bold, e.g., $RULE$), and minuscule letters to denote elements of this matrix, $\mathbf{a}$. Elements always contain indexes to specify the element, e.g., $\mathbf{a}_{i,j}$. Indexes denote the dimensions of matrices. We use indexes for matrices (e.g., $\mathbf{A}_{i,j}$) only when we would like to specify the dimensions of the matrix explicitly. In this section we also use sets of indexes. For example, if we have matrix $\mathbf{A}_{i_1,i_2,i_3}$ with elements $\mathbf{a}_{i_1,i_2,i_3}$ for brevity we write $\mathbf{A}_I$, where $I = \{i_1, i_2, i_3\}$. Let IJK denote any combination of indexes from sets $I = \{i_1, i_2\}$, $J = \{j_1, j_2\}$, and $K = \{k_1, k_2\}$ preserving the order for every set (e.g., $i_1, j_1, j_2, k_1, i_2, k_2$) and $\overline{IJK}$ denote the ordered set of indexes where all indexes from I are followed by all indexes of J and then are followed by all indexes of K (e.g., $i_1, i_2, j_1, j_2, k_1, k_2$).

In the paper we use summation of matrixes, two types of multiplication [8] and a special *diag* operation, defined as follows.

Definition 1. *Let $\mathbf{A}_I$ and $\mathbf{B}_I$ be two matrices of $|I|$ dimensions. Then $\mathbf{C} = \mathbf{A} + \mathbf{B}$ is also an $|I|$-dimensional matrix with values $\mathbf{c}_I = \mathbf{a}_I + \mathbf{b}_I$;*

Definition 2. *The multidimensional matrix outer product is multiplication of every element of one matrix by every element of another matrix. The multidimensional matrix outer product $\mathbf{A}_I \otimes \mathbf{B}_K$ is a multidimensional matrix $\mathbf{C}_{\overline{IK}}$ every element of which is computed as: $\mathbf{c}_{\overline{IK}} = \mathbf{a}_I * \mathbf{b}_K$.*

Definition 3. *The multidimensional matrix inner product is defined as a contracted multiplication of elements of both matrixes with different indexes. The multidimensional matrix inner product $\mathbf{A}_{IJ} \times \mathbf{B}_{JK}$ is a multidimensional matrix $\mathbf{C}_{\overline{IK}}$ every element of which is computed as: $\mathbf{c}_{\overline{IK}} = \sum_{\forall j \in J} \mathbf{a}_{IJ} * \mathbf{b}_{JK}$.*

In our work, the elements of all matrices belong to a specific domain of results $\Re = \{\varnothing, \boxtimes, \perp, \top\}$ (we also use $\Re' = \{\varnothing, \top\} \subset \Re$). Thus, we have to define the "$*$" and "$\sum$" (or "$+$") operation on the elements of the domain to be able to apply operations defined in Definitions 1, 2, and 3 on matrices.

Definition 4. *Multiplication ("$*$") and addition ("$+$" or $\sum$) operations are defined by two corresponding tables*

$$
\begin{array}{c|cccc}
\text{``$*$''} & \top & \perp & \boxtimes & \varnothing \\
\hline
\top & \top & \perp & \boxtimes & \varnothing \\
\perp & \perp & \perp & \boxtimes & \varnothing \\
\boxtimes & \boxtimes & \boxtimes & \boxtimes & \varnothing \\
\varnothing & \varnothing & \varnothing & \varnothing & \varnothing
\end{array}
\qquad
\begin{array}{c|cccc}
\text{``$+$''} & \top & \perp & \boxtimes & \varnothing \\
\hline
\top & \top & \top & \top & \top \\
\perp & \top & \perp & \perp & \perp \\
\boxtimes & \top & \perp & \boxtimes & \boxtimes \\
\varnothing & \top & \perp & \boxtimes & \varnothing
\end{array}
\tag{4}
$$

In the following we will use multiplication of elements to indicate whether a specific element should be considered (e.g., whether a rule should check the value of an attribute). The addition operation indicates how considered elements should be combined (e.g., whether there is at least one value of an attribute satisfying a rule). Since a rule may result in either $\perp$ and $\top$ if applicable we will never meet the addition of $\perp$ and $\top$ values in our work. For the final combination of rules (see Equation 3) we use a simple algorithm, which allows access if at least one rule allows it (similar to deny-unless-permit rule-combining algorithm in XACML). One observation is useful here: if the access control system only specifies when access is allowed ($\top$) and simply ignores the rest ($\varnothing$) then denoting $\top$ as 1 and $\varnothing$ as 0 we get usual boolean operations for *and* and *or*.

Proposition 1. *The operations defined in Definition 4(proofs are in Appendix):*

1. *$*$ and $+$ are commutative,*
2. *$*$ and $+$ are associative,*
3. *$*$ is distributive over $+$.*

Proposition 2. *Let us have three multidimensional matrices $\boldsymbol{A}_{IJK}$, $\boldsymbol{B}_{IML}$, $\boldsymbol{C}_{JMN}$ and $IJK \cap IML \cap JMN = \emptyset$.*

1. *$(\boldsymbol{C} \times \boldsymbol{B}) \times \boldsymbol{A} = \boldsymbol{C} \times (\boldsymbol{B} \times \boldsymbol{A})$.*
2. *$(\boldsymbol{C} \times \boldsymbol{B}) \times \boldsymbol{A} = ((\boldsymbol{C} \times \boldsymbol{A}) \times \boldsymbol{B})^{T(K;L)}$, where $\boldsymbol{D}^{T(K;L)}$ means transposition, i.e., interchanging of positions, of indexes from set K and L preserving order.*

Two points can be derived from Proposition 2. First, if $I = \emptyset$ then $\mathbf{B} \times \mathbf{A} = \mathbf{B} \otimes \mathbf{A}$, since there are no indexes for contraction. Second, changing the order of matrices does not change the elements of the resulting matrix, but only the order of dimensions.

Finally, we define an operation *diag* which reduces a set of dimensions J of a matrix to one dimension, using only the diagonal elements of J.

Definition 5. *Let $\boldsymbol{A}$ be a multidimensional matrix with dimensions IJK, where $\forall j_t \in J, t = 1...k$ for some finite k. Then,*

$$
C = diag_J(\boldsymbol{A}_{IJK}) \; ; \; c_{I\{j\}J} = a_{I\{j_1=j, j_2=j, ..., j_k=j\}K}
\tag{5}
$$

Proposition 3. *If matrix $\boldsymbol{A}_{IJK}$ has only one dimension $J = \{j_1\}$, then $diag_J(\boldsymbol{A}_{IJK}) = \boldsymbol{A}_{IJK}$*

4   Matrix Form for ABAC Model

In this section we define a matrix form of ABAC similar to the one used for the role engineering [2]. This form is required in order to explicitly link such entities as subject, object and allowed actions. In other words, at the end of the modelling process we should get a way to easily say which subject has access to which object and which action it is allowed to do on the object. Note, that although a similar link also exists in XACML policies, it is not explicit. For example, a rule which says that *every user from an IT department which has a permanent position may access a document of a project* requires some analysis before saying that John may access description of work of the project.

4.1   Attribute Assignment

First we consider attribute assignments to different entities specified by functions $ATTR$ in Equation 1. Let A be a set of all attributes considered in the system, i.e., for an $a \in A$ we have one corresponding $ATTR$. All functions $ATTR$ may be considered as a three dimensional boolean matrix:

$$\mathbf{ATTR} = (\mathbf{attr}_{i_e,i_a,i_d}); \ \mathbf{attr}_{i_e,i_a,i_d} \in \{\varnothing, \top\} \qquad (6)$$
$$i_e = 1...|E|; \ i_a = 1...|A|; \ i_d = 1...|D_{i_a}|$$

which assigns $\top$ to an element if an entity $i_e = index(e)$ $e \in E$ has the value of an attribute $i_a = index(a)$ $a \in A$ equals to $i_d = index(d)$ $d \in D_{i_a}$. By $index()$ we mean a function which returns the index of the input. In the following we simply write $i_a = a$. It is very important to note, that in our notations *indexes also explicitly point out the kind of dimension they refer to*. This means, that we should not care much about the order of indexes, since we always can identify them using the name of indexes.

When we define a matrix we first specify its name and element with all indexes, e.g., $\mathbf{ATTR} = (\mathbf{attr}_{i_e,i_a,i_d})$, then we specify the values of the elements $(\mathbf{attr}_{i_e,i_a,i_d} \in \{\varnothing, \top\})$ and finally, we list the ranges of indexes. Indexes of matrices, also denoting the dimensions, are specified as i with a subscript pointing to the nature of the dimension, e.g., i_e denotes an entity dimension. Because of this explicit binding the order of indexes is not important in our work. If we want to refer to a specific element we assign values to the indexes: $\mathbf{attr}_{i_e="John",i_a="age",i_d="22"}$. We use superscripts in brackets for subjects (s), objects (o), actions (act) to denote the corresponding subsets of entities (e.g., $S = E^{(s)} \subseteq E$), attributes (e.g., $A^{(s)} \subseteq A$), and domains $(D^{(s)} \subseteq D)$. We also use a specific notation for indexes used only for a subset of entities (e.g., index (i) for attributes (a) of subjects (s) is i_{a_s}).

Note, that for computational reasons values are considered specific for each attribute (i.e., D_{i_a}). In this case, one dimension of $\mathbf{ATTR}$ matrix will be different for different attributes, but this deviation from the classical representation of matrices does not affect further discussion (but simply requires careful consideration when operations on matrices are defined). Also note, that although some attribute domains may be infinite we almost always can make them finite, e.g., a domain of natural numbers may be truncated at some value (e.g., 100) and a special value (≥ 100) added to denote the other possible values.

We would like to separate subjects, objects, actions as it is done in XACML (w.l.o.g., we do not use environmental types):

$$\mathbf{ATTR}^{(s)} = (\mathbf{attr}^{(s)}_{i_s,i_{a_s},i_{d_s}}); \ \mathbf{attr}^{(s)}_{i_s,i_{a_s},i_{d_s}} \in \{\varnothing, \top\}; \tag{7}$$

$$i_s = 1...|E^{(s)}|; \ i_{a_s} = 1...|A^{(s)}|; \ i_{d_s} = 1...|D^{(s)}_{i_{a_s}}|$$

$$\mathbf{ATTR}^{(o)} = (\mathbf{attr}^{(o)}_{i_o,i_{a_o},i_{d_o}}); \ \mathbf{attr}^{(o)}_{i_o,i_{a_o},i_{d_o}} \in \{\varnothing, \top\} \tag{8}$$

$$i_o = 1...|E^{(o)}|; \ i_{a_o} = 1...|A^{(o)}|; \ i_{d_o} = 1...|D^{(o)}_{i_{a_o}}|$$

$$\mathbf{ATTR}^{(act)} = (\mathbf{attr}^{(act)}_{i_{act},i_{a_{act}},i_{d_{act}}}); \ \mathbf{attr}^{(act)}_{i_{act},i_{a_{act}},i_{d_{act}}} \in \{\varnothing, \top\} \tag{9}$$

$$i_{act} = 1...|E^{(act)}|; \ i_{a_{act}} = 1...|A^{(act)}|; \ i_{d_{act}} = 1...|D^{(act)}_{i_{a_{act}}}|$$

4.2 Rules Definition

Now we need to specify the matrix for $RULE$ functions. For this matrix we need a set of rules $r \in R$. Every element of set R relates to one $RULE$ function. We also need to capture the parameters of the $RULE$ function. Here we would like to recall, that for precise description of the parameters of $RULE$ function we need to use triples: entity-attribute-value (or separate triples for subject, object, and action; see Equations 7, 8, and 9). We define **RULES** matrix for $RULE$ functions (using the specified triples) as:

$$\mathbf{RULES} = (\mathbf{rules}_{i_r,i^1_{a_s}...i^{n_s}_{a_s},i^1_{d_s}...i^{n_s}_{d_s},i^1_{a_o}...i^{n_o}_{a_o},i^1_{d_o}...i^{n_o}_{d_o}} \tag{10}$$

$$_{,i^1_{a_{act}}...i^{n_{act}}_{a_{act}},i^1_{d_{act}}...i^{n_{act}}_{d_{act}},i^1_e...i^{n_a}_e,i^1_a...i^{n_a}_a,i^1_d...i^{n_a}_d});$$

$\mathbf{rules}_{...} \in \{\bot, \top, \boxtimes, \varnothing\}; \ i_r = 1...|R|;$

$\forall i_{a_s} = 1...|A^{(s)}|; \ \forall i_{d_s} = 1...|D^{(s)}|; \ \forall i_{a_o} = 1...|A^{(o)}|; \ \forall i_{d_o} = 1...|D^{(o)}|;$

$\forall i_{a_{act}} = 1...|A^{(act)}|; \ \forall i_{d_{act}} = 1...|D^{(act)}|;$

$\forall i_e = 1...|A|; \ \forall i_a = 1...|A|; \ \forall i_d = 1...|D|;$

The amount of dimensions in this most generic case is $1 + 2 * n_s + 2 * n_o + 2 * n_{act} + 3 * n_a$, where n_s, n_o, n_{act}, n_a are the maximal number of attributes for subject, object, action and bound attributes used for one rule. Since every rule must be stated for a subject-object-action triple, n_s, n_o, n_{act} cannot be 0, while bound attributes are optional and n_a can be 0. For example, if we want to express a policy, consisting of one rule stating that *"a user may get an object only if the sum of his money at present and possible credit is higher than the cost of the object"*, we have 2 attributes of a subject (money the user has now, possible amount of a credit for the user) and 1 attribute of an object (cost of this object), one for action (type of action, e.g., "get"). Thus, $n_s = 2$, $n_o = 1$, and $n_{act} = 1$ and the amount of dimensions to consider is $1 + 4 + 2 + 2 = 9$.

It is important to note, that in practice, the table itself should not be defined manually (unless specific modifications are required), but should be either automatically derived from the defined rules or found using attribute mining with different heuristic methods (and then transformed to usual XACML policies).

Now, we are able to see which subject-object-action triples satisfy defined rules. For this purpose we need to provide the required parameters for $RULE$ functions. In the matrix form, this means that we need to multiply **RULES** matrix by a corresponding $\mathbf{ATTR}^{(s)}$, $\mathbf{ATTR}^{(o)}$, $\mathbf{ATTR}^{(act)}$ or/and **ATTR** matrix one time for a required attribute. Thus, in the case of the previous example, we need to multiply **RULES** by $\mathbf{ATTR}^{(s)}$ twice, by $\mathbf{ATTR}^{(o)}$ once, and once by $\mathbf{ATTR}^{(act)}$. First we consider bound attributes (we hide all dimensions which do not take part in the multiplication for brevity). Let **RULES_RES'**, **RULES_RES''**, **RULES_RES'''** be three auxiliary matrices.

$$\mathbf{RULES\_RES'} = (...((\mathbf{RULES} \times \mathbf{ATTR}) \times \mathbf{ATTR}) \times ... \times \mathbf{ATTR}) = \quad (11)$$
$$\mathbf{RULES} \times (\mathbf{ATTR})^{n_a}$$

$$\mathbf{rules\_res'}_{i_r,...} = (\sum_{\forall i_e^1,...,i_e^{n_a}} \sum_{\forall i_a^1,...,i_a^{n_a}} \sum_{\forall i_d^1,...,i_d^{n_a}} \mathbf{rules}_{i_r,...,i_e^1...i_e^{n_a},i_a^1...i_a^{n_a},i_d^1...i_d^{n_a}} *$$

$$* \mathbf{attr}_{i_e^1...i_e^{n_a},i_a^1...i_a^{n_a},i_d^1...i_d^{n_a}}$$

By $(\mathbf{ATTR})^{n_a}$ we denote the outer matrix product applied several times to the same matrix (Proposition 2 for the proof). Although i_e^1 and i_e^2 denote the same dimension (i.e., entity) they refer to different entity-attribute-value triples. Thus, we cannot apply contraction to them computing $(\mathbf{ATTR})^{n_a}$.

When we multiply the resulting matrix on $\mathbf{ATTR}^{(s)}$, $\mathbf{ATTR}^{(o)}$, $\mathbf{ATTR}^{(act)}$ we do not simply do contraction of all indexes, as it was in case of **ATTR** matrix. In these cases the dimensions denoting the entities to which the attributes belong to (i.e., free dimensions) are added to the resulting matrix. Since we would like to consider one subject, one object and one type of actions we should take the elements with the same indexes (i.e., apply $diag$ function to $I_s = \{i_s^t | t = 1...n_s\}$).

$$\mathbf{RULES\_RES''}_{i_r,i_s,...} = diag_{I_s}(\mathbf{RULES\_RES'} \times (\mathbf{ATTR}^{(s)})^{n_s}) = \quad (12)$$
$$diag_{I_s}(\mathbf{RULES\_RES'''}_{i_r,i_s^1...i_s^{n_s},...})$$

Let $I_o = \{i_o^l | l = 1...n_o\}$ and $I_{act} = \{i_{act}^k | k = 1...n_{act}\}$. The matrix of result of rules for subjects performing actions on objects is:

$$\mathbf{RULES\_RES}_{i_r,i_s,i_o,i_{act}} = diag_{I_{act}}(diag_{I_o}(diag_{I_s}(\mathbf{RULES} \times (\mathbf{ATTR})^{n_a})$$
$$\times (\mathbf{ATTR}^{(s)})^{n_s}) \times (\mathbf{ATTR}^{(o)})^{n_o}) \times (\mathbf{ATTR}^{(act)})^{n_{act}} \quad (13)$$

Note, that according to Proposition 2 the order of multiplication changes only the order of dimensions in the resulting matrix, but not the elements of the matrix. Thus, we may apply multiplications in any order, respecting the converged dimensions and $diag$ operations.

4.3   Access Control Matrix

We know the decisions for every rule with respect to a subject-object-action triple. A Policy Decision Point (PDP) should consider all rules and provide the final decision. Let $\mathbf{PDP}_{i_r}$ be the final rules-combining matrix, used by PDP to combine all rules and make an authorisation decision.

$$\mathbf{PDP} = (\mathbf{pdp}_{i_r}); \ \mathbf{pdp}_{i_r} = \top; i_r = 1...|R| \tag{14}$$

In short PDP simply collects all authorisation decisions provided by the rules. Thus, the access control matrix ($\mathbf{ACM}$), which defines which action a subject may perform on which objects, can be found as follows:

$$\mathbf{ACM}_{i_s,i_a,i_{act}} = \mathbf{RULES\_RES}_{i_r,i_s,i_a,i_{act}} \times \mathbf{PDP}_{i_r} \tag{15}$$

4.4   Example

Assume we consider access control policies for a hospital. We consider four subjects $S = \{John, Peter, Paul, Eve\}$ which may access three records $O = \{rec1, rec2, rec3\}$ of three different patients $\{Ada, Felix, Rebecca\}$. In this small hospital there are only two departments (surgery and infection departments $(D_1^{(s)} = \{sur, inf\})$ in which two doctors $\{John, Peter\}$ and two nurses $\{Paul, Eve\}$ work $(D_2^{(s)} = \{doctor, nurse\})$. Three rules are defined for the access control:

1. *rule1: Doctors are allowed to write all patient records*;
2. *rule2: Nurses from surgery are not allowed to write the record of Rebecca*;
3. *rule3: Anyone from infection department can read all records*;

We see, that there are 2 attributes of subjects we should consider: the role in the hospital and the department the subject belongs to. For object we have only one parameter: name of the patient. Finally, we would like to consider two types of access: read and write. Thus, the three matrixes of attributes are:

$$\mathbf{ATTR}^{(s)} = \begin{matrix} s_1(John) \\ s_2(Peter) \\ s_3(Paul) \\ s_4(Eve) \end{matrix} \left[\begin{bmatrix} doctor & nurse \\ \top & \varnothing \\ \top & \varnothing \\ \varnothing & \top \\ \varnothing & \top \end{bmatrix} \begin{bmatrix} sur & inf \\ \top & \varnothing \\ \varnothing & \top \\ \top & \varnothing \\ \varnothing & \top \end{bmatrix} \right] \tag{16}$$

$$\mathbf{ATTR}^{(o)} = \begin{matrix} rec1 \\ rec2 \\ rec3 \end{matrix} \begin{bmatrix} Ada & Felix & Rebecca \\ \top & \varnothing & \varnothing \\ \varnothing & \top & \varnothing \\ \varnothing & \varnothing & \top \end{bmatrix} \quad \mathbf{ATTR}^{(act)} = \begin{matrix} act_w \\ act_r \end{matrix} \begin{bmatrix} write & read \\ \top & \varnothing \\ \varnothing & \top \end{bmatrix}$$

$$\tag{17}$$

Now we need to model $\mathbf{RULES}$ table. We see that we use at most 2 attributes of a subject in rule 2. As for attributes of object and action we use only one of them maximum. Thus, we need $1 + 2 * 2 + 1 * 2 + 1 * 2 = 9$ dimensions. On the other hand, since we have only one attribute for object and action we can skip dimensions for them, using only the dimensions for the values of these attributes. We also see that rules 1 and 2 are defined for the *write* action only, when rule 3 is defined for the *read* action. Thus, all elements related to rule 3 for action *read* and 1 and 2 for action *write* are $\varnothing$. Therefore, for brevity, we show only the meaningful parts of the **RULES** matrix (see Equation 18).

If one wants to read Equation 18 we propose to start unwrapping it from the middle. Consider any smallest two-by-two matrix with elements easily singled out in any place of the **RULES** matrix. Every row in such matrix means either the role of the subject (marked as "role" for the corresponding rows) or the department a subject belongs to (we use a mark "dep" for the corresponding rows). The columns contain values of role ("doctor" for the first $(d_1^{(s)})$ row and "nurse" for the second $(d_2^{(s)})$) or department $(d_1^{(s)} = sur$ or $d_1^{(s)} = inf)$. We should not be scared by different meanings (and even different size) of domains for different rows, since we will apply operations only with rows of similar kind. Thus, the element of the matrix says whether a subject with a specific value of an attribute is allowed to do something.

Next, we see these smallest two-by-two matrices are combined in other two-by-two matrices (for which the smallest matrices are just elements). We see that the rows again denote roles and departments, and columns denote possible values. We should not be surprised because we considered the attributes of subjects twice. Finally, we see that there are three such higher rank matrices (for Ada, Felix, and Rebecca), which are obviously related to the only object attribute we consider and its three possible values.

Naturally, we should not forget about action value dimension (*read* and *write*) and three rules. Thus, Equation 19 shows the final matrix. This matrix explicitly indicates how a rule is applied to a subject-object-action triple.

Finally, the **ACM** matrix is (using Equation 15):

$$\mathbf{ACM}_{i_s, i_o, i_{act}} = \tag{20}$$

$$\begin{bmatrix} & \begin{bmatrix} & act_w & \\ & s_1 & s_2 & s_3 & s_4 \\ rec1 & \top & \top & \varnothing & \varnothing \\ rec2 & \top & \top & \varnothing & \varnothing \\ rec3 & \top & \top & \bot & \varnothing \end{bmatrix} & \begin{bmatrix} & act_r & \\ & s_1 & s_2 & s_3 & s_4 \\ & \varnothing & \top & \varnothing & \top \\ & \varnothing & \top & \varnothing & \top \\ & \varnothing & \top & \varnothing & \top \end{bmatrix} \end{bmatrix}$$

5   Engineering Access Control Policies for ABAC

Role engineering is a set of activities which aim at finding a suitable set of roles, user-role and role-permission assignments. Role engineering is considered either like a top-down approach (when external information about possible roles exists) or as a bottom-up approach, usually referred to as role mining [4, 2]. Similar to role engineering for RBAC we specify a policy engineering problem for ABAC. Here we focus on an attribute mining problem.

RULES = $\hspace{11cm}$ (18)

$$
\left[
\begin{array}{l}
\left[
\begin{array}{c}
d_1^{(act)} = write;\, rule1 \\
\end{array}
\right] \\
\end{array}
\right.
$$

$d_1^{(o)} = Ada$ $\qquad$ $d_2^{(o)} = Felix$ $\qquad$ $d_3^{(o)} = Rebecca$

$role$ $\qquad\qquad$ $role$ $\qquad\qquad$ $role$

rule1:

$d_1^{(o)} = Ada$:

role	doctor		nurse	
	$d_1^{(s)}$	$d_2^{(s)}$	$d_1^{(s)}$	$d_2^{(s)}$
role	$\top$	$\top$	$\varnothing$	$\varnothing$
dep	$\varnothing$	$\top$	$\varnothing$	$\varnothing$

role	sur		inf	
	$d_1^{(s)}$	$d_2^{(s)}$	$d_1^{(s)}$	$d_2^{(s)}$
role	$\top$	$\top$	$\top$	$\varnothing$
dep	$\varnothing$	$\varnothing$	$\varnothing$	$\varnothing$

$d_2^{(o)} = Felix$:

role	doctor		nurse	
	$d_1^{(s)}$	$d_2^{(s)}$	$d_1^{(s)}$	$d_2^{(s)}$
role	$\top$	$\top$	$\varnothing$	$\varnothing$
dep	$\varnothing$	$\top$	$\varnothing$	$\varnothing$

role	sur		inf	
	$d_1^{(s)}$	$d_2^{(s)}$	$d_1^{(s)}$	$d_2^{(s)}$
role	$\top$	$\top$	$\top$	$\varnothing$
dep	$\varnothing$	$\varnothing$	$\varnothing$	$\varnothing$

$d_3^{(o)} = Rebecca$:

role	doctor		nurse	
	$d_1^{(s)}$	$d_2^{(s)}$	$d_1^{(s)}$	$d_2^{(s)}$
role	$\top$	$\top$	$\varnothing$	$\varnothing$
dep	$\varnothing$	$\top$	$\varnothing$	$\varnothing$

role	sur		inf	
	$d_1^{(s)}$	$d_2^{(s)}$	$d_1^{(s)}$	$d_2^{(s)}$
role	$\top$	$\top$	$\top$	$\varnothing$
dep	$\varnothing$	$\varnothing$	$\varnothing$	$\varnothing$

$d_1^{(act)} = write;\, rule2$

$d_1^{(o)} = Ada$ $\qquad$ $d_2^{(o)} = Felix$ $\qquad$ $d_3^{(o)} = Rebecca$

$d_1^{(o)} = Ada$:

role	doctor		nurse	
	$d_1^{(s)}$	$d_2^{(s)}$	$d_1^{(s)}$	$d_2^{(s)}$
role	$\varnothing$	$\varnothing$	$\varnothing$	$\varnothing$
dep	$\varnothing$	$\varnothing$	$\varnothing$	$\varnothing$

role	sur		inf	
	$d_1^{(s)}$	$d_2^{(s)}$	$d_1^{(s)}$	$d_2^{(s)}$
role	$\varnothing$	$\varnothing$	$\varnothing$	$\varnothing$
dep	$\varnothing$	$\varnothing$	$\varnothing$	$\varnothing$

$d_2^{(o)} = Felix$:

role	doctor		nurse	
	$d_1^{(s)}$	$d_2^{(s)}$	$d_1^{(s)}$	$d_2^{(s)}$
role	$\varnothing$	$\varnothing$	$\varnothing$	$\varnothing$
dep	$\varnothing$	$\varnothing$	$\varnothing$	$\varnothing$

role	sur		inf	
	$d_1^{(s)}$	$d_2^{(s)}$	$d_1^{(s)}$	$d_2^{(s)}$
role	$\varnothing$	$\varnothing$	$\varnothing$	$\varnothing$
dep	$\varnothing$	$\varnothing$	$\varnothing$	$\varnothing$

$d_3^{(o)} = Rebecca$:

role	doctor		nurse	
	$d_1^{(s)}$	$d_2^{(s)}$	$d_1^{(s)}$	$d_2^{(s)}$
role	$\varnothing$	$\varnothing$	$\varnothing$	$\varnothing$
dep	$\varnothing$	$\varnothing$	$\bot$	$\varnothing$

role	sur		inf	
	$d_1^{(s)}$	$d_2^{(s)}$	$d_1^{(s)}$	$d_2^{(s)}$
role	$\varnothing$	$\bot$	$\varnothing$	$\varnothing$
dep	$\varnothing$	$\varnothing$	$\varnothing$	$\varnothing$

$d_2^{(act)} = read;\, rule3$

$d_1^{(o)} = Ada$ $\qquad$ $d_2^{(o)} = Felix$ $\qquad$ $d_3^{(o)} = Rebecca$

$d_1^{(o)} = Ada$:

role	doctor		nurse	
	$d_1^{(s)}$	$d_2^{(s)}$	$d_1^{(s)}$	$d_2^{(s)}$
role	$\varnothing$	$\varnothing$	$\varnothing$	$\varnothing$
dep	$\varnothing$	$\top$	$\varnothing$	$\top$

role	sur		inf	
	$d_1^{(s)}$	$d_2^{(s)}$	$d_1^{(s)}$	$d_2^{(s)}$
role	$\varnothing$	$\varnothing$	$\top$	$\top$
dep	$\varnothing$	$\top$	$\top$	$\top$

$d_2^{(o)} = Felix$:

role	doctor		nurse	
	$d_1^{(s)}$	$d_2^{(s)}$	$d_1^{(s)}$	$d_2^{(s)}$
role	$\varnothing$	$\varnothing$	$\varnothing$	$\varnothing$
dep	$\varnothing$	$\top$	$\varnothing$	$\top$

role	sur		inf	
	$d_1^{(s)}$	$d_2^{(s)}$	$d_1^{(s)}$	$d_2^{(s)}$
role	$\varnothing$	$\varnothing$	$\top$	$\top$
dep	$\varnothing$	$\top$	$\top$	$\top$

$d_3^{(o)} = Rebecca$:

role	doctor		nurse	
	$d_1^{(s)}$	$d_2^{(s)}$	$d_1^{(s)}$	$d_2^{(s)}$
role	$\varnothing$	$\varnothing$	$\varnothing$	$\varnothing$
dep	$\varnothing$	$\top$	$\varnothing$	$\top$

role	sur		inf	
	$d_1^{(s)}$	$d_2^{(s)}$	$d_1^{(s)}$	$d_2^{(s)}$
role	$\varnothing$	$\varnothing$	$\top$	$\top$
dep	$\varnothing$	$\top$	$\top$	$\top$

$$\mathbf{RULES\_RES}_{i_r,i_s,i_o,i_{act}} = diag_{i_{act}}\left(diag_{i_o}\left(diag_{i_s}\left(\mathbf{RULES}\times(\mathbf{ATTR}^{(s)})^2\right)\right.\right.$$
$$\left.\left.\times\,\mathbf{ATTR}^{(o)}\right)\times\mathbf{ATTR}^{(act)}\right) = \hspace{3cm} (19)$$

rule1	act_w				act_r			
	s_1	s_2	s_3	s_4	s_1	s_2	s_3	s_4
rec1	$\top$	$\top$	$\varnothing$	$\varnothing$	$\varnothing$	$\varnothing$	$\varnothing$	$\varnothing$
rec2	$\top$	$\top$	$\varnothing$	$\varnothing$	$\varnothing$	$\varnothing$	$\varnothing$	$\varnothing$
rec3	$\top$	$\top$	$\varnothing$	$\varnothing$	$\varnothing$	$\varnothing$	$\varnothing$	$\varnothing$

rule2	act_w				act_r			
	s_1	s_2	s_3	s_4	s_1	s_2	s_3	s_4
rec1	$\varnothing$	$\varnothing$	$\varnothing$	$\varnothing$	$\varnothing$	$\varnothing$	$\varnothing$	$\varnothing$
rec2	$\varnothing$	$\varnothing$	$\varnothing$	$\varnothing$	$\varnothing$	$\varnothing$	$\varnothing$	$\varnothing$
rec3	$\varnothing$	$\varnothing$	$\bot$	$\varnothing$	$\varnothing$	$\varnothing$	$\varnothing$	$\varnothing$

rule3	act_w				act_r			
	s_1	s_2	s_3	s_4	s_1	s_2	s_3	s_4
rec1	$\varnothing$	$\varnothing$	$\varnothing$	$\varnothing$	$\varnothing$	$\top$	$\varnothing$	$\top$
rec2	$\varnothing$	$\varnothing$	$\varnothing$	$\varnothing$	$\varnothing$	$\top$	$\varnothing$	$\top$
rec3	$\varnothing$	$\varnothing$	$\varnothing$	$\varnothing$	$\varnothing$	$\top$	$\varnothing$	$\top$

Definition 6. *(Basic Attribute Mining Problem (AMP)). Given a set of users S, a set of objects O, a set of possible actions Act, a set of considered attributes A and a subject-object-action assignments **ACM**, find:*

- *$ATTR$ matrix (or $ATTR^{(s)}$, $ATTR^{(o)}$, $ATTR^{(act)}$ matrixes), i.e., the values of the attributes entities have.*
- *$RULES$ matrix, i.e., the amount of attributes used at most for one rule (n_s, n_o, n_{act}, n_a); attributes required for every rule; the bound entities the attributes belong to; values of all attributes required for satisfaction of rules;*

The basic AMP is a general and complex problem. One may find a large number of variations of this problem assuming, that some information is available. In some cases, **ATTR** matrix may be known (or at least partially known) a priori [3]. For example, such information as age of a subject, its position in the organisation, time of access, a level of criticality of an object may be known in advance. Naturally, in these cases also the domains of the attributes are known. Sometimes also n_s, and n_o values may be known (or assumed, or bound). Further elaborations on the problem, similar to [4] are possible.

The problem for engineering access control policies in more general, can be defined similar to AMP, where instead of (or in addition to) **ACM** any relevant information is available (e.g., business process, a structure of an enterprise, possible losses of incorrect access granting/denying, etc).

5.1   Role Engineering in ABAC

Here we show how your model can be adapted for RBAC case. RBAC assigns a role to a subject and then maps the role with permissions. Here we consider RBAC without hierarchy, i.e., so called flat model [9]. Although ABAC model also is able to use the role as an attribute, it also may work with other attributes (also attributes of an object, an action, etc.) without the need to create (often meaningless) auxiliary roles.

First, RBAC model specifies only when a subject is allowed (i.e., "Permit" decision) to access an object, and uses "deny" decision otherwise. It does not use neither explicit "deny" decision, i.e., ⊥, nor "undefined", i.e., ⊠. Thus, all operations for matrices are boolean "and" for multiplication and "or" for addition.

There is one attribute we should consider in this case: a role of a subject. Thus, $ATTR^{(s)}$ contains 3 dimensions, one of which, i.e., attribute dimension, has only one element, e.g., "role". Therefore, w.l.o.g., we may consider this matrix as a two-dimensional boolean matrix which assigns subjects to their roles. $ATTR^{(o)}$ and $ATTR^{(act)}$ are simple unit matrices, which simply state, that an object is this object and an action is this action. We need only one attribute for specifying this. Thus, these two matrixes are also two dimensional unit matrices (similar to Section 4.4).

RULES matrix needs $1 + 2 * 1 + 2 * 1 + 2 * 1 + 3 * 0 = 7$ dimensions. Note, that attribute dimensions for subject, object, and action have only one element and we can remove them for simplicity. Thus, we have 4 domains: role, attribute values of subject (i.e., role values), attribute values of object (i.e., objects themselves), attribute values of action (i.e., actions themselves).

Let M be a set of permissions $m \in M$, which may be defined as a pair of an object and an action allowed on the object [2, 4]. We may define two matrices **RULES_PERM** and **PERM_OBJ** to break **RULES** in two:

$$\textbf{RULES\_PERM} = (\textbf{rule\_perm}_{i_r, i_{d_s}, i_m}); \ \textbf{rule\_perm}_{i_r, i_{d_s}, i_m} \in \{\varnothing, \top\}$$

$$\textbf{PERM\_OBJ} = (\textbf{perm\_obj}_{i_m, i_{d_o}, i_{d_{act}}}); \ \textbf{perm\_obj}_{i_m, i_{d_o}, i_{d_{act}}} \in \{\varnothing, \top\}$$

$$i_r = 1...|R|; \ i_{d_s} = 1...|D_1^{(s)}|; \ i_m = 1...|M|; \tag{21}$$

$$i_{d_o} = 1...|D_1^{(o)}|; \ i_{d_{act}} = 1...|D_1^{(act)}|;$$

$$\textbf{RULES} = \textbf{RULES\_PERM} \times \textbf{PERM\_OBJ} \tag{22}$$

$$\textbf{rules}_{i_r, i_{d_s}, i_{d_o}, i_{d_{act}}} = \sum_{\forall i_m} \textbf{rule\_perm}_{i_r, i_{d_s}, i_m} * \textbf{perm\_obj}_{i_m, i_{d_o}, i_{d_{act}}}$$

We define **RULES_PERM** matrix as a three-dimensional binary matrix assigning $\top$ to the element $\textbf{rule\_perm}_{i_r = r, i_{d_s} = d^{(s)}, i_m = m}$ if a rule r assigns a permission m to every subject with an attribute value (i.e., a role) $d^{(s)} \in D_1^{(s)}$, and $\varnothing$ otherwise. Let also define **PERM_OBJ** which assigns $\top$ to an element $\textbf{perm\_obj}_{i_m = m, i_{d_o} = d^{(o)}, i_{d_{act}} = d^{(act)}}$ if a permission m is defined for the attribute value of object (i.e., object itself) $d^{(o)} \in D_1^{(o)}$ and for the attribute value of action (i.e., action itself) $d^{(act)} \in D_1^{(act)}$.

In this section we do not strictly keep the required order of indexes to simplify the discussion. This relaxation does not violate the computation, but only changes the order of indexes (which can be always changed by transposition).

First, consider Equation 19:

$$\textbf{RULES\_RES}_{i_r, i_s, i_o, i_{act}} = ((\textbf{RULES} \times \textbf{ATTR}^{(s)}) \times \textbf{ATTR}^{(o)}) \times \textbf{ATTR}^{(act)}$$

$$= (\textbf{RULES\_PERM} \times \overline{\textbf{PERM\_OBJ}}_{i_m, i_o, i_{act}}) \times \textbf{ATTR}^{(s)} \tag{23}$$

We removed *diag* operation, since there is only one dimension which has to be considered in all three cases (see Proposition 3). For representation reasons, we use the same matrix **PERM_OBJ** for the result of operation (**PERM_OBJ** $\times$ **ATTR**$^{(o)}$) $\times$ **ATTR**$^{(act)}$ denoted as $\overline{\textbf{PERM\_OBJ}}_{i_m, i_o, i_{act}}$, since in fact, this operation does not change the matrix (because **ATTR**$^{(o)}$ and **ATTR**$^{(act)}$ are unit matrices), but simply renames the dimensions i_{d_o} to i_o and $i_{d_{act}}$ to i_{act}.

Now, we add the result of Equation 23 to Equation 15:

$$\textbf{ACM} = (\textbf{RULES\_PERM} \times \overline{\textbf{PERM\_OBJ}}) \times \textbf{ATTR}^{(s)}) \times \textbf{PDP} \tag{24}$$

$$= (\textbf{RULES\_PERM} \times \textbf{PDP}) \times \textbf{ATTR}^{(s)}) \times \overline{\textbf{PERM\_OBJ}}$$

Let **ROLE_PERM** = **RULES_PERM** $\times$ **PDP**. We see that this two dimensional matrix assigns value $\top$ if there is a role-permission assignment, and $\varnothing$ otherwise.

In role engineering matrix $\overline{\text{PERM\_OBJ}}$ is considered given. Now, let $\mathbf{ACM} = \mathbf{ACM'} \times \overline{\text{PERM\_OBJ}}$, where $\mathbf{ACM'}$ is a two-dimensional boolean matrix which means that a subject has a permission. Then, we have, that:

$$\mathbf{ACM} = \mathbf{ACM'} \times \overline{\text{PERM\_OBJ}}$$

$$= (\mathbf{RULES\_PERM} \times \mathbf{PDP}) \times \mathbf{ATTR}^{(s)}) \times \overline{\text{PERM\_OBJ}} \tag{25}$$

$$\mathbf{ACM'} = \mathbf{ROLE\_PERM} \times \mathbf{ATTR}^{(s)} \tag{26}$$

Equation 26 is equivalent to RBAC model in a matrix form $\mathbf{UPA} = \mathbf{UA} \times \mathbf{PA}$ [2] which has a number of solutions presented in the literature [4–6].

6   Discussion

The first and the main point we would like to discuss is the complexity of the proposed approach. Indeed, usage of multidimensional matrices makes the computation and representation hard. The following observation is useful here. Looking to the matrixes required for role engineering to take into account one attribute (role) we see that there is a need to specify all subject-role and role-permission relations, which also highly increase complexity of the task, but this approach proved to be useful in practice. In this paper we proposed a technique, which should take into account any number of attributes. Thus, we should not be surprised of increased complexity. Moreover, the process of creation of such matrices should be automatic, rather than manual. Furthermore, computations can be significantly simplified by marking the dimensions, which contain only $\varnothing$ symbols. Thus, there is no need to compute every operation, but only meaningful ones.

One thing we did not consider in the paper is different environmental conditions. Thus, access may be allowed during the working hours, and forbidden in other time of the day. XACML uses environmental attributes together with attributes of subject, object and action for analysis of access requests. Such dimension can be easily added to the model using the same strategy we apply for subjects, objects, and actions.

XACML also assumes, that sometimes several subjects may be considered for one access request. In this case we cannot simply apply *diag* function in Equations 13, but must consider all subjects separately. In this article we do not consider this sophisticated case, but simply note, that our framework requires little changes for taking this possibility into account.

All in all, the proposed model is the first attempt, to our knowledge, to define the policy engineering problem for ABAC using a matrix form. Thus, we acknowledge that the proposed model may be simplified (e.g., in defining **RULES** matrix) especially, when specific cases of policy engineering problem for ABAC are used (e.g., when we model RBAC case). We also acknowledge that the model can be tuned to address the features of XACML more accurately (e.g., addition of policies and policy sets), but the current version had the main goal to take into account the core concept of ABAC.

7   Related Work

ABAC is a generalisation of traditional access control models [1]. It is capable to express complex security policies and it is resistant against scalability problems which occur when a number of subjects accessing a resource is enormous. The recent Usage Control (UCON) model [10, 11] is also an example of ABAC. The specific features of the UCON model are mutable attributes and continuous policy enforcement. The XACML framework [7], an open standard proposed by OASIS, is an example of application-independent ABAC for access control. In fact, XACML provides a language to express security policies and an enforcement architecture. Recently, XACML was extended in order to encode usage control policies and to support the continuous policy enforcement, i.e., it was extended to capture features of the UCON model [12].

There were several attempts to formalise ABAC. A logic-based formalisation of ABAC for access control is given in [13]. Crampton and Morisset proposed a formal language for ABAC that addresses the same problem space as XACML [14]. UCON formalisation based on temporal logic can be found in [15]. Martinelli et al. [16] proposed a formalisation based on a process algebra. Although these approaches are fruitful for automatic evaluation and enforcement of security policies, they are not suitable for management of attributes and for engineering of security policies. Management of mutable attributes in UCON was addressed in [17, 18]. Authors described how the decision making is affected by uncertain attribute values and how often mutable attributes should be refreshed.

Benefits, shortcomings, and open problems of ABAC models were surveyed in [19]. Attribute design and engineering of security policies were named as problems there. Our paper gives a first step towards defining and solving them.

We consider role mining in RBAC as a starting point. Indeed, the role can be just considered as an attribute, and roles to permissions assignments as a policy. Role mining, introduced in 2003 [3], gained a lot of attention in last years and a large number of different approaches to the problem were proposed [4–6, 20]. The authors of these approaches showed that it is convenient to use matrices for defining formally and solving automatically the role-mining problems.

8   Conclusions and Future Work

In this work we made the first steps towards defining access control policy engineering problem for ABAC. We proposed a matrix-based formalisation of the ABAC model. Our formalisation is based on the XACML standard, which should help adapting our findings in practice. We provided the basic attribute mining problem definition using our formalisation and showed how this bottom-up approach can be generalised for the policy engineering problem for ABAC.

In the paper we specified a large number of directions for future work: closer adaptation of the approach to XACML, considering policies and rules-combining algorithms; elaboration of policy engineering problem for ABAC; reducing the complexity of the model, etc. Naturally, solutions for the specified problem is the main future work we need to consider.

References

1. Jin, X., Krishnan, R., Sandhu, R.: A unified attribute-based access control model covering dac, mac and rbac. In: Cuppens-Boulahia, N., Cuppens, F., Garcia-Alfaro, J. (eds.) DBSec 2012. LNCS, vol. 7371, pp. 41–55. Springer, Heidelberg (2012)
2. Frank, M., Buhmann, J.M., Basin, D.: On the definition of role mining. In: Proceedings of SACMAT 2010, pp. 35–44. ACM (2010)
3. Kuhlmann, M., Shohat, D., Schimpf, G.: Role mining - revealing business roles for security administration using data mining technology. In: Proceedings of SACMAT 2003, pp. 179–186. ACM (2003)
4. Vaidya, J., Atluri, V., Guo, Q.: The role mining problem: Finding a minimal descriptive set of roles. In: Proceedings of SACMAT 2007, pp. 175–184. ACM (2007)
5. Vaidya, J., Atluri, V., Guo, Q.: The role mining problem: A formal perspective. ACM TISSEC 13(3), 27:1–27:31 (2010)
6. Lu, H., Vaidya, J., Atluri, V., Hong, Y.: Constraint-aware role mining via extended boolean matrix decomposition. IEEE TDSC 9(5), 655–669 (2012)
7. OASIS: extensible access control markup language (xacml) version 3.0. (January 2013),
   http://docs.oasis-open.org/xacml/3.0/xacml-3.0-core-spec-os-en.pdf
8. Solo, A.M.G.: Multidimensional matrix mathematics. In: Proceedings of the World Congress on Engineering, vol. I, pp. 1824–1850. International Association of Engineers, Newswood Limited (2010)
9. Ferraiolo, D.F., Sandhu, R., Gavrila, S., Kuhn, D.R., Chandramouli, R.: Proposed nist standard for role-based access control. ACM TISSEC 4(3), 224–274 (2001)
10. Sandhu, R., Park, J.: Usage control: A vision for next generation access control. In: Gorodetsky, V., Popyack, L.J., Skormin, V.A. (eds.) MMM-ACNS 2003. LNCS, vol. 2776, pp. 17–31. Springer, Heidelberg (2003)
11. Lazouski, A., Martinelli, F., Mori, P.: Usage control in computer security: A survey. Elsevier Computer Science Review 4(2), 81–99 (2010)
12. Lazouski, A., Mancini, G., Martinelli, F., Mori, P.: Usage control in cloud systems. In: Proceedings of ICITST 2012, pp. 202–207. IEEE (2012)
13. Wang, L., Wijesekera, D., Jajodia, S.: A logic-based framework for attribute based access control. In: Proceedings of FMSE 2004, pp. 45–55. ACM (2004)
14. Crampton, J., Morisset, C.: PTaCL: A language for attribute-based access control in open systems. In: Degano, P., Guttman, J.D. (eds.) POST 2012. LNCS, vol. 7215, pp. 390–409. Springer, Heidelberg (2012)
15. Zhang, X., Parisi-Presicce, F., Sandhu, R., Park, J.: Formal model and policy specification of usage control. ACM TISSEC 8(4), 351–387 (2005)
16. Martinelli, F., Mori, P., Vaccarelli, A.: Towards continuous usage control on grid computational services. In: Proceedings of ICAS-ICNS 2005. IEEE (2005)
17. Krautsevich, L., Lazouski, A., Martinelli, F., Mori, P., Yautsiukhin, A.: Integration of quantitative methods for risk evaluation within usage control policies. In: Proceedings of ICCCN 2013. IEEE (to appear, 2013)
18. Krautsevich, L., Lazouski, A., Martinelli, F., Yautsiukhin, A.: Cost-effective enforcement of access and usage control policies under uncertainties. IEEE Systems Journal 7(2), 223–235 (2013)
19. Sandhu, R.S.: The authorization leap from rights to attributes: maturation or chaos? In: Proceedings of SACMAT 2012, pp. 69–70. ACM (2012)
20. Colantonio, A., Di Pietro, R., Ocello, A., Verde, N.V.: Mining stable roles in RBAC. In: Gritzalis, D., Lopez, J. (eds.) SEC 2009. IFIP AICT, vol. 297, pp. 259–269. Springer, Heidelberg (2009)

Appendix

Proposition 4. *The operations defined in Definition 4:*

1. *$*$ and $+$ are commutative,*
2. *$*$ and $+$ are associative,*
3. *$*$ is distributive over $+$.*

Proof. The commutative property of $+$ and $*$ follows from the symmetry of tables defined in Definition 4.

Now consider associative property of "$+$": a+(b+c)=(a+b)+c

- Let $a = \top$, then the result of the left part is $\top$ is annihilating element of "$+$". The right part is also $\top$, since now we apply annihilating element twice ($a + b$ and $((a + b) + c)$). Note, that this means that if any of the elements is $\top$ then the property holds.
- Let $a = \bot$ and $b \neq \top$ and $c \neq \top$. Then $\bot$ is an annihilating elements for the three values which are left and we have the same reasoning that we had for $a = 1$.
- Let $a = \boxtimes$ $b \neq \top$ $b \neq \bot$ and $c \neq \top$ and $c \neq \bot$. Now $\boxtimes$ is an annihilating element
- Let $a = b = c = \varnothing$. Trivial.

The proof for associative property of "$*$" is the same but we should do it other way round (start with $\varnothing$, which is annihilating element for "$*$").

Now we prove that $a * (b + c) = a * b + a * c$.

- Let $a = \top$. From the definition of multiplication operator we see that $1*d = d$ for any d. Thus, $a * (b + c) = b + c = a * b + a * c)$.
- Let $a = \bot$ and $a * c$ and $a * b$ can be anything, but $\top$.
  - Let b be either $\top$ or $\bot$ then $a * b = \bot$. $\bot$ plus anything, but $\top$ is equals to $\bot$. Then, since $b + c = \bot$ or $b + c = \top$ then $a * (b + c) = \bot$. The same holds for $c = \top$ or $c = \bot$
  - Let $b = \boxtimes$. Then $a*b = \boxtimes$ and $b+c = \boxtimes$. Thus, $a*(b+c) = \boxtimes = a*b+a*c$. The same holds for $c = \boxtimes$
  - Let $b = c = \varnothing$. $a * (b + c) = \varnothing = a * b + a * c$.
- Let $a = \boxtimes$.
  - Let b be either $\top$ or $\bot$ or $\boxtimes$ then $a * b = \boxtimes$. Moreover, $b + c =$ is $\top$ or $\bot$ or $\boxtimes$ and $a * (b + c) = \boxtimes$. Since $a * c$ is either $\boxtimes$ or $\varnothing$, then $a*b+a*c = \boxtimes = a * (b+c)$. The same holds if c is either $\top$ or $\bot$ or $\boxtimes$;
  - Let $b = c = \varnothing$. $a * (b + c) = \varnothing = a * b + a * c$.
- Let $a = \varnothing$. From the definition of multiplication operator we see that $\varnothing * d = \varnothing$ for any d. Thus, taking into account that $\varnothing + \varnothing = \varnothing$ $a * (b+c) = \varnothing = a * b + a * c)$.

$\square$

Proposition 5. *Let us have three multidimensional matrices* $\boldsymbol{A}_{IJK}$, $\boldsymbol{B}_{IML}$, $\boldsymbol{C}_{JMN}$ *and* $IJK \cap IML \cap JMN = \emptyset$.

1. $(\boldsymbol{C} \times \boldsymbol{B}) \times \boldsymbol{A} = \boldsymbol{C} \times (\boldsymbol{B} \times \boldsymbol{A})$.
2. $(\boldsymbol{C} \times \boldsymbol{B}) \times \boldsymbol{A} = ((\boldsymbol{C} \times \boldsymbol{A}) \times \boldsymbol{B})^{T(K;L)}$, *where* $\boldsymbol{D}^{T(K;L)}$ *means transposition, i.e., interchanging of positions, of indexes from set* K *and* L *preserving order.*

Proof.   Let the result of $(\mathbf{C} \times \mathbf{B}) \times \mathbf{A}$ be $\mathbf{D}$.

$\mathbf{d}_{\overline{NLK}} = \sum_{IJ}(\sum_M(\mathbf{c}_{JMN} * b_{IML}) * \mathbf{a}_{IJK}) = \sum_{IJM}((\mathbf{c}_{JMN} * \mathbf{b}_{IML}) * \mathbf{a}_{IJK})$ by distributive property of $*$ over $+$. Now, by the associative property of $*$ we have, that $\sum_{IJM}((\mathbf{c}_{JMN} * \mathbf{b}_{IML}) * \mathbf{a}_{IJK}) = \sum_{JM}(\mathbf{c}_{JMN} * \sum_I(\mathbf{b}_{IML} * \mathbf{a}_{IJK})) = \mathbf{d}_{\overline{NLK}}$ by distributive property of $*$ in reverse direction and commutative property of $+$. Thus, $\mathbf{D} = \mathbf{C} \times (\mathbf{B} \times \mathbf{A})$

We also see, that $\mathbf{d}_{\overline{NLK}} = \sum_{IJM}((\mathbf{c}_{JMN} * \mathbf{b}_{IML}) * \mathbf{a}_{IJK}) = \sum_{IJM}((\mathbf{c}_{JMN} * \mathbf{a}_{IJK}) * \mathbf{b}_{IML}) = \sum_{MN}(\sum_J(\mathbf{c}_{JMN} * \mathbf{a}_{IJK}) * \mathbf{b}_{IML}) = \mathbf{d'}_{\overline{NKL}}$. Thus, $\mathbf{D'}_{\overline{NKL}}^{T(K;L)} = ((\mathbf{C} \times \mathbf{A}) \times \mathbf{B})^{T(K;L)} = \mathbf{D}_{\overline{NLK}}$ $\square$

Proposition 6. *If matrix* $\boldsymbol{A}_{IJK}$ *has only one dimension* $J = \{j_1\}$, *then* $diag_J(\boldsymbol{A}_{IJK}) = \boldsymbol{A}_{IJK}$

Proof.   Let $\mathbf{C} = diag_J(\mathbf{A}_{IJK})$, then $\mathbf{c}_{I\{j\}J} = \mathbf{a}_{I\{j_1=j\}K} = \mathbf{a}_{I\{j\}K}$. Thus, $\mathbf{C} = \mathbf{A}_{IJK}$ $\square$

Author Index

Bender, Jens   17

Eckert, Claudia   53

Fischlin, Marc   17

Koeberl, Patrick   36
Krautsevich, Leanid   85
Kügler, Dennis   17

Lazouski, Aliaksandr   85
Li, Jiangtao   36

Martinelli, Fabio   70, 85
Matteucci, Ilaria   70

Saracino, Andrea   70
Sgandurra, Daniele   70
Stumpf, Frederic   53

Tomlinson, Allan   1

Velten, Michael   53

Wessel, Sascha   53
Wu, Wei   36

Yap, Jiun Yi   1
Yautsiukhin, Artsiom   85